T0062418

GOD GETS THE GLORY!

WHO WILL WIPE MY TEARS AWAY?

My Story
Written By: Evangelist Earlina Denise Gilford- Weaver

Order this book online at www.trafford.com
or email orders@trafford.com

Most Trafford titles are also available at major online book retailers.

Printed in Victoria, BC, Canada.

ISBN: 978-1-4269-3008-9 (sc)
ISBN: 978-1-4269-3009-6 (hc)

Library of Congress Control Number: 2010903617

*Our mission is to efficiently provide the world's finest, most comprehensive book publishing
service, enabling every author to experience success. To find out how to publish your book, your
way, and have it available worldwide, visit us online at www.trafford.com*

Trafford rev. 4/14/2010

www.trafford.com

North America & international
toll-free: 1 888 232 4444 (USA & Canada)
phone: 250 383 6864 ♦ fax: 812 355 4082

I
DEDICATE
This Book To

My lord and savior Jesus Christ

My Mother & Father who is gone home to be with the lord

My Babe Sister Snetha Davis you got a story to tell! Tell it!!!

My Children that love me through it all!!! I Love You, Theresa, Floyd, Jermaine, Stephanie

My Husband, for knowing how to hold on until the change comes

Mother Williams for being my ROCK

Minister Burt Williams for just being you!

My Aunt Pat, My Grandmother Katie, My Cousin Peaches

My Adopted sister Leslie Scott for being a good sister

A good Sister in the Lord that believed in the Ministry in me Minister Rochelle Dawson

For all the people that help me jump over the mess by being the mess!

For Seeing Through God's Eyes Ministry' it isn't over tell God says its Over!!

Special Dedication to my Brother Curtis I Miss you!!

To a Special mother that God sent my way Corneisha Jones who told me to make a stand for something.

Angel W/Extra Blessings & Gods Chosen Angels Out Reach Ministry

The ministry that the lord had in me all the time, for giving birth right when I needed a friend who restored my soul and gave me true purpose and courage to keep on standing throw the storms and hurricanes which made me a sparkle in the eye of all them tears and a twinkle star in God heart!!!

And to the Angel God sent in my life to sing the life I truly had inside of me a purpose a plan and my destiny when life seem like was all over for me the Lord sent me an Angel that helped the tears to flow in the right direction. Thank you for being who God says you are Minister Darlene Brown.

This book is to reach all types of situations, all young and old children of god, the lost and found, this is life, I pray this book helps you through any storms in your life, so that you can come out of them hidden dark closets the enemy has hidden you in!

After reading about my life, I hope and pray that this will be a step for you to make toward your victory, and bring you closer to the one and only true love of your life, "Jesus Christ" and to come clean with god and allow him to restore the true beauty that Satan has colored ugly!! So that you will be able to take off that mask of shame, fame, and game! And give god the glory for giving you the power to KNOW WHO I S GOING TO wipe them tears away!!!

REVELATION: CHAPTER 21 VERSE 7

I am going to starting my story with the age I could remember, lots of us like to talk about what People or family have told us things that happened in our life, but the word of God tells us to speak only things that are seen and not things that we really don't know the facts. I don't want to write hear say only the facts, I never wanted to be a false witness to any thing rather I believe it or not, so here it goes! I am telling what I know, what I have experience in my life, up till this point. If you got kids put them to bed, if you got company talk to them later, if your phone rings let the answering machine get it, sit in a comfortable seat cut off the TV and be ready to feel that God is real!!

Here it is the truth and nothing but the truth in Jesus Name!

I was 8 years old I really never remember my parents only my grandmother and a few aunts and uncles and hand full of cousins. At this time of my life I was living with my grandmother, she had raised her kids and now some of her grandkids, grandma always took us to church and this is when I started hearing about a man name Jesus and God in heaven that we pray to when we need him, at this time of my age they would tell us to pray for things that we want that are good or something we wanted God to change. Especially if things are bad! So I always kept this in my heart and mind. I always wanted to know where and who my parents really were, but we really never talked about it, but I did know their names, so I kept a lot to myself. So growing up with a lot of thoughts to myself was very hard, because I really never knew how to talk to God about it, especially when I could not see him. So as time went by I was about 9 or 10 years old my grandmother would take us over one of our aunts house to stay a lot because she loved to go to bingo, her and my aunt would go and a couple of uncles would care for us, baby-sit, and their type of babysitting was not good it was bad! They would do bad things to me and my cousins and my little sister, they would come into our bedrooms and touch us in places that were bad places, that my grandmother would say that was precious to God, and they would make us touch them in places that felt bad. Sometimes they would pull our legs apart and put something in, and it would hurt. It would hurt so bad that I would pray to God to make them stop. I would pray all the time to God for it would all go away. Make them stop God, and bring something good because this was bad, it would make me shed tears all the time, but he never did. And it continue on and on and on our uncles would threaten us, telling us that we better not tell, because no one would believe us. And we would be sent away to strangers that would do worst things to us, because my mother was a prostitute and my father was a drunk and they did not want me, So we kept it to ourselves, me and my cousin would talk about it among ourselves, and I would talk to my little sister about it. Even my brother could not help me, even through he tried so many times, but they were older and stronger than him. They would beat him up all the time and tell my grandmother that he was bad so he would get in trouble all the time. But my brother never stop trying to help me! No matter what it cost him! As time went by I started to act bad so God could bring good, then my grandmother started to get sick she was caring for us and it got to be to much for her. And by then I was to much for her to handle and I had a favorite aunt that I was so close too, I use to think she was my mother but she was just my aunt she helped my grandmother with us a lot but I that was not enough.

But I was glad to get away from them monsters my uncles. I started getting visits from a man that was always drunk, and my grandmother let me know that he was my father but he was scary but to tell you the truth I did not care, because if I could go with him it would be better than being with my uncle. But my grandmother would not allow him to take me, my grandma would send him off seeing that I was kind of scared of him, and his actions, and there was something he did in the past to me, he had kidnap me and put me in a cage as a baby in a basement, I was told this, but I have memories of this sometimes I don't know how old I was at that time.

He would always say I am your father girl don't be scared of me! In away I was still scared, father or not, his action was crazy. My grandmother never let me go with him, But as time went on grandma had to let someone else care for us, I was scared to go somewhere else, so one day she told us that our mother was coming to get us, I really wanted to meet her, but my brother hated her, and I did not want him to be mad at me so I would act like I hated her to. Even through I was so sad and wanted my mother to take me away from the monster's in my grandmother house, but I love my brother so much I did not want to hurt him, so I would do what he did and say what he say, but our grandmother said we had to go with her even through we said we did not want to go, grandma was tired and she needed some rest, so my brother would get into so much trouble that he got sent away for a while just so he would not go with our mother, but me and my sister went with our mother, she seemed to be very nice and she would buy us lots of stuff, so I was happy, no one coming into the bedrooms to mess with us I was about 10 at this time every thing was okay until our mother start letting these men come over, they were no good, bad men like my uncles, they were left at the house with me and my sister when our mother went to work, and they would look at me so weird and then the touching started to happen again, they would force them self on me and I was scared for my little sister I would see her cry when they would go by her so I would take her place, I had enough tears myself for me and her both, and I did not want her to go through the mess we went through over grandma. So I would protect my sister like my brother would do me and let my mother boyfriends touch me instead, I cried and cried and cried for God to please save me. Since God did not help I had to do anything so they would not hurt my baby sister. My mother would come home and I would tell her that I did not like her boyfriend because they were bad and mean to me and my sister, she would get mad at me like she hated me and told me to stop lying, I was not going to mess up her life, I better be glad she came and got me and if I keep lying then she was going to send me away, one day she slapped me across the face with a hot comb that you straighten your hair with, because I kept telling her what they would do to me. So I just stayed quite and kept what ever happened to myself, I got beat every time her boyfriends said I was mean to them. So I let them do what ever. I knew if I fought back like I did I would get beat any way or I would get killed, I see why my brother hated her where is this God my grandmother said you can pray to when things get bad? I guess this was not bad enough for God to hear my prayers, so as time went by, I got rebellious and act up, I hated my mother all she cared about is money and her men, it seemed like they would give her money just to leave the house so they could rape her daughter, I wondered if she knew? And just did not care, or what.

So I started stealing, lying and talking back to my mother and I would runaway all the time, It seem like the streets were safer than grandma house and my mother house, finally I got into so Much trouble that it headed me into being awarded to the state, where they placed me into a juvenile detention home since God would not help my tears to stop maybe the courts would. I stayed in a group homes until I got into foster care and went into about 23 different places in all, I was about 13 thru the 15 years old and believe me it was only 3 good homes I had out of all the foster care homes, that was okay to live in. I had to endue so much abuse such as name calling because I was dark skin, beatings because of other people kids, sexually and being molested by these so called foster mothers husbands, brothers, sometimes their uncles or their older sons. Sometimes I would not eat they would send me to bed with out dinner at times, I had to clean up the whole house by myself, I had got into lots of fights with their children because they would talk about my mother and father, for some strange reason I could not explain why I would get mad because my parents never cared anything about me, if they did they would not allow these things to happen to me but in my heart I loved my mom and dad and wanted dearly to have an relationship with them, strange but real. I can remember this one foster home I got sent to I was about 14 and it was in Canton Ohio, I was happy to go their maybe because it was not in the hometown I stayed in, and I thought maybe the people would be different maybe only bad things happen where I lived and God would help me somewhere else, This home was big and nice the foster home parents had three children two girls and one boy one was around my age, for about one month everything was great I was so happy, God heard my cry, because every night I would get scared and the foster mother would come and hold me and wipe my tears away with a purple small cloth, I was so scared to get close to her, I was scared to love her or her kids, I loved the one foster sister I had, she was so nice we would go to church together and sing in the choir it was so nice, then one day I came home from church and my make believe family was a nightmare my foster mother wanted me to go in the basement and get some things for her, she had to go to the store and my one foster sister went with her and my foster brother was out with his friends and my one foster sister was in her room, she was a special need child, she had Autism, so she stayed in her room a lot so I was left their to care for her, my foster dad always stayed in the basement I never knew why, they never was in the same bedroom, he was always in the basement working and drinking so he lived down in the basement. We never had a relationship like my foster mother and foster sibling, so I walked down in the basement and I was singing a song we had learn at church and he ask me to come here, I was not really scared because he never done anything to me and I was living their for about 2 months, so I went to see what he wanted and he ask me to help hold some kind of board down for him and I did he started asking me question like do I like boys or men? And I was a pretty black girl, and I had a nice body shape, I was so scared to answer him, I started shaking and told him I had to get back up stairs before they come home, I had to do something for my foster mom, but he grabbed me and said they will not be back for a while, so be quite and stop my crying, he started saying I read your files and you was already damage goods, and no one else would have you, and they would not believe you if you tell my wife, we will send you back from where you came from,

I was so upset with God I did not understand why the lord would allow this to happen in another Town and they would do worst to me. Why did my past follow me here! So here I go again my tears has return I was so ashamed that God never love me enough to not let these tears return. I guess adults just don't know how to love or treat a child like me. Broken, rejected, neglected, molested, ugly, black, a one big failure, this is all they had seen in me, just a messed up kid and just too much work to keep. Well I stayed in this foster home for 6 months I starting getting into trouble so much and my foster mother could not deal with it any more because she said that it would effect her children, so her and the monster in the basement decided to send me away after he suggested that I sleep in the basement, so I would not be poison to his girls, I refuse to sleep down there, and I grabbed a knife to offend myself from going into the basement. So the child service people came and they tried to talk to my foster mother to give me another chance, so we talked and I told them why I was acting out because I did not want to go in the basement because her husband had hurt me, just like he said, she would not believe me she hated me and made them take me away! So here I am again going back to the city of death. And into another place where I stayed in, they called me names, cut my hair to make me look like a boy, mentally and physically abuse me, and made me wear ugly clothes, the only time I dressed nice was when the social workers come and do a home visit. This is the only time I felt pretty on the outside, but after the visit the nightmare on everyone street I stayed with. But I had my share of tears that no one never seen and that was the ones on the inside that no one could get to, not even me could wipe them away. I always remember to pray from my grandmother, I don't know why I did but I always wanted to obey my Grandmother, so I prayed and prayed and prayed till I could not pray anymore for God to please wipe my tears away, then I just gave up on the God my grandmother would talk about. So I tried to kill myself in the group homes they took me too, by taking a lot of pills I was 14 years old when they put me in a mental hospital. This is when I realize no one will wipe my tears away; I am an unwanted child why did God allow me to be born? Cause I was a child of the devil, I had to be because my grandmother said God loves his children, to turn his back on me like this, I could not be one of his children. Was this my punishment for my mother mistakes? for her life being not right and had me? Is this why God could not love me? Or wipe my tears away? I had no life to look forward to, no one will ever love me unless I allow everyone to touch me in ways I never wanted to be touch. Should I allow them to do this to me? so I can get love? I ask God but he never answered me. What kind of God is this that my Grandma said is Love, what is Love? Is it really a thing that you let all men do bad things to you? I know in the bible when I was little, my grandma always told me that God loves virgins and he will bless me if I keep myself for when I get married, so did God hate me because my uncles did things to me? Was it my fault? I was too young to make them stop, didn't God know this? I kept telling myself over and over again. If my tears never get wipe then I will drown. So why live to see my life fail? I will never be nothing that is what my mom always said to me, she said women would never be alone or need money if they use what God gave them.

She said that between a woman legs is money to her riches, I hated to hear her talk like that to me, I never wanted my little sister to be raised by her, I always said to myself when I get big I was going to go back and get my babe sister. But God would never allow me to with the way my life was going. Maybe I would have a chance if the drunk that said he was my father come and get me, or if my brother gets big he would come and get me. It seems like they were the only ones that cared for me, maybe they would wipe my tears away. While I was in the mental hospital it was workers that watch you all the time they kept me so drugged up I really did not know who I was at times. Then one night it was a guy on shift that would always be nice to me, and bring me extra snacks he was nice I thought to myself but deep down inside I knew he wanted some thing, so I tried to hang myself, I just did not like how he touched me and before it got physical I rather take my life then to allow it to happen again. But it happen any way and the workers would not believe me, because the drugs make you say things that was in your mind, this is what they would tell me, but this was not in my mind their kept on telling me that, because of the drama in my life, they said I would think that every man that touch me would be the wrong way in my mind. God still would not let me die! Because I ended up in the hospital and they saved me. From what? Not hell, cause I was in hell. Then I met a lady in the hospital that was so different from any one I have met, she was a patient to at the hospital, she was two doors down from my room and she would here me scream and cry and would come to my room and hold me until I would fall a sleep, who was this lady that cared for me? Why do she care? And she would ask the nurses and doctors about me, and how could she take me home, she wanted to be my mother not a foster mother, but my adopted mother. I asked God why do she want a skinny, ugly, black, messed up, a child with lots of problems, don't she know what a hot mess I was. I was confused, I really did not trust no body, no adults because I knew they did not love me, so why do this woman want me? So I would not get close to this woman because I was scared to trust again or open my heart up to anyone, even through I wanted love and wanted someone to wipe my tears away, but

I was scared to be with her especially if she had a husband, male friend, brothers, nephews, uncles, sons or even grandfathers or cousins that were men. But at this time she got the information from the child services, but they had located my real father, he was staying with his sister, my aunt wanted me to live with them. I was glad but scared because I did not know these people at all. But what can be worst go with my real family or try this nice lady at the hospital. But I really had no choice, so they took me to my aunts house and there was that same man that would come over my grandma house drunk, this man was really my father now wonder I was messed up look where I came from, a mom that was a prostitute and a father that was a drunk. I lived with them for awhile my aunt was so nice I liked her so much, she was an angel in the sky in my eyes, but she was gone a lot because of her religion, I had lots of cousins and me and my cousin the girl was very close we did a lot together my father drank so much, we really never spent time together, I did not like the way his breathe smelled he was always trying to kiss me and call me my mom nick name he had for her. My father was there to watch us a lot but I did not care we had a lots of freedom.

Finally I got to see my brother he was eighteen and he fought to look for me, he was looking all over for me, he was locked up a lot, and he stayed into lots of trouble because he had no one. he never knew who his real father was and my mother cared less, so he hung with the wrong crowd of people. He had an older girlfriend and he was doing okay, he bought me so many clothes and other things, my brother loved me so much and asked me all the time was I happy and I told him yes, because my auntie was great. I was about 15 years old I had 8 more months before I turned 16, my little sister was still living with our mother in New York I was so scared for her, I knew what my mother had done to me so I knew my sister was going to be messed up, so I would at least pray for her maybe God would help her. and if she had any tears he would wipe them away. I was getting sick a lot because I had asthma and it was hard for me to breathe my tonsils were swelling so I had to go in the hospital to get them out. I was sick one night my father came in drunk and laid down next to me calling me my mothers name he was talking so crazy I got scared but I knew he was out of his mind. I did not want to believe that my own father would do anything to me, so I would try to push him out of my bed, but he was heavy and strong and my throat was so sore I could not scream for help, he kept on grabbing me hard and then started calling me my mother name again saying I was his wife, no one can have me but him, I tried to lift him off me but he was to heavy I was to weak I tried screaming again, but no one was home every one was at the temple I could not go because I was sick and my father was watching me, my nightmare began again my own father raped me, did he know it was me? because he kept calling me my mother. I begged God to kill me, so I took all my aunts painkillers and other pills I could find, I went to the hospital and they pumped my stomach what is God's problem? Haven't I suffered enough? I ended back in another group home. I was there for about three months. And that real nice lady came and got me, and told me that no one else would ever hurt me again and she had adopted me she was my mother and every thing was going to be okay, and for some strange reason I believed her. She told me that child services had called her and asked her if she still wanting to adopt me I was 16 and would be 17 in 3 months what do she want with me I was to big for any one to want me, I wanted to go with my brother he was old enough but because of his back ground and criminal record they would not let me go. So I went with the nice lady. I was bitter with life. mad at the world I did not care about any thing any more I was so sad I did not want to smile their was nothing to smile about everything in my life was dark. All the tears I have was flowing in the inside, my heart was drowning, so I went to my new home, my case worker said it will be better this time, I heard this so much I was wondering who was they fooling their self, because they was not fooling me, the house was nice she had beautiful things, she have two boys and two girls one my age and the others were younger and their were happy to have me. I was still full of anger and did not trust no one especially boys and men's, but I said if it happen again I don't care because my body was numb, I just did not care any more.

The home was exciting lots of family and friend in and out just like a family that was normal. I fitted Right in, me and my adopted sisters were great together never fought just was crazy about each other, I loved my little adopted sister and little brother just like a real family I always wanted. We played, cried, and act bad all together, never a difference was made between us, no man in the house, that was great just my adopted mother had a male friend, but she never let him stay at the house, she had brothers they came and left they were nice, when she yelled at me she yelled at her kids the same, when she spared the rod on me she did her kids, called me names and put me on punishment just like she did her kids, they got it more than me, she would spoil me a lot, I was so happy to be in a normal home, but still had tears that would not go away, No matter what and how my new family tried to wipe them. Even through my grandma house had monster's in it, I loved being with my grandma because she never used bad words at us, she took us to church to learn how to be right and love each other and learn about a man name Jesus who died for my sins, and I missed her she was to sick and got to old to raise us, I was not mad at her I loved her, I wanted to tell her so much what my uncles did but I was to scared to let her know, my cousins never said anything to her or my little sister, so I kept my mouth closed, but I did tell my adopted mom every thing she tried to wipe my tears away but it was so much going on, it was hard for me to feel her wipes. Maybe this is how people raise their kids I thought. Call them bad words and names, beat them when they act up, I don't really know but I did not care, I stayed here until I got 17 and believe it or not no one ever touched me in a bad way, my adopted mother said to me if any one try to touch me let her know, and she would kill their behinds. She was tough and no one messed with her, not even her sisters or brother's and she had her man in check. So it was a normal family to me, the best I can ask for. So I did not care about going to church or pray to a God that never heard or seen my tears, my adopted mother took care of it for me. My father would try to come see me, still drinking and acting crazy, she never let him get close to me or see me, not even my real mother she made sure she protected me from all danger, my real brother always came to see me they loved him and excepted him as family. He was her son and my adopted brothers and sisters were his family, they treated him how they did me. I guess this is love. Maybe everyone shed tears, so my tears did not matter, inside I felt something was missing I really wanted to see my real mother no matter what she had did, I loved her for some crazy reason I loved my adopted mother but she was not my real mother. And I did not what to hurt her feelings by telling her I wanted to see my real mother and my little sister so bad, I just wanted to know if my little sister was okay, I always told her I would protect her and be there for her. I was scared she was going through what I have been through and who was there to wipe her tears away? This time I was being stable and it seemed like God was letting me off the hook, maybe he cared for me enough to stop the pain in my life. Even though everyone at this home seemed to love me and treat me so good, sometimes I was treated better than her own children.

Now it is 1976 and I was pregnant, and did not know what to do in case something like this ever happens? How do I handle it? Or should I feel anything? I was so scared, so I hid it from everyone I was 17 years old at this time and was going to be 18 years old in 5 months, I kept it to myself, so I decided to runaway before anyone finds out. Where would I go? So I started asking my adopted mother could I go see my real mother she kept telling me no, then one day she told me yes, so my real brother did not like our real mother but he knew I wanted to see her so he wanted to make me happy, so he went looking for her for me she was living on the other side of town with a new man and my little sister, she had moved back from New York. And was living here for a while, I guess she did not care to find us, but we found her, And she was living in a real nice home and had lots of nice stuff, I was mad and my brother hated her so much, he was not talking to her he went back and sat in his car while I visit her and my sister. My little sister was 15 years old, and my mother looked so nice and pretty how can a nice looking lady be so ugly inside I asked myself? We talked ok my little sister wanted me to see her room so I did, she had a nice room better than I ever had or imaged, she had nice cloths and lots of toys, I was kind of jealous of her and felt a little hate, but it was so nice to see her, so I shook it off, then as we were leaving her room she grabbed my hand and said please spend the night with me, it wasn't what she said, but how she said it! I felt scared for her she had that fear tears voice I know very well, this kind of voice I had, so I told her I would be back if our mother let me stay. So we went down stairs and a man walked in the door he was looking at me like he wanted something, I felt his spirit was not right so I ask my mother could my sister spend the night with me, she said no I don't like that lady you live with. In a very nasty voice. So I ask could I spend the night before my mother could answer that man did, he said sure you can, you can stay as much as you want to, looking at me like I was something to eat. So when my brother took me back I told my brother I believe something was going on with our little sister, he act like he really did not care, my brother always hid his feelings, he never talked to me about our mother or past only that he hated her and that would make me so sad. So we got back over my adopted mothers house and I asked her could I spend the night over my mothers house she said no, I begged her and she still said no, but I was so scared for my little sister I could not put her teary voice out of my head, so I decided to runaway to live with my real mother, plus I was scared to let my adopted mother know I was pregnant anyway, so I left the house that night I had to be about three or four months along, but I wore big cloths from head to toe, I did not want to dress like a girl or nice, because I was scared someone might want sex from me, so I dressed like a boy all the time, with big clothes on so no one knew I was pregnant, so I arrived at my real mothers house and she answered the door I told a lie so I could stay, I told her that my adopted mother brother was trying to mess with me, so she let me stay. My little sister had a big smile on her face my mom and her man talked about it and he said I could stay because it was his house.

So I went into my sister room and put my things up that I had with me, my mother said we need to get you some new cloths because you look a hot mess, I told her that was okay but she said you need to look like a woman not a man, you need sexy cloths but I did not want her to see that I had a little stomach, cause she would know that I was having a child. So my sister and me went in her room and talked I asked her did that man ever touch Her? But she was to scare to tell me the truth she would tear up and say no, but I knew he had to do something. So I told her I was about to be eighteen in about 8 months and she could come and live with me. We went to sleep talking, nothing happen that night but a lot of arguing between my mother and that man. I was there at least a week I was sad because I did not want to hurt my adopted mother so I wrote her a letter to let her know why I really left and I love her and I will be back to see her. So as time went on two weeks my mother took me shopping but I act like I was sick, I did have asthma so I act like I could not breathe so she took me home. That night she had to go to work and left me and my sister home with her man, I did not like his short bright skin self he was so ugly and thought he was sharp. He calls my little sister in his bedroom and she was scared so I went with her, he asked me what do you want? I said nothing, I am just here with my sister so you can tell her what you want in front of me, he got mad and told my sister to leave and I stay. He got up and closes the door and said if I want to be living here I had to earn my stay like my sister. I did not care what he did to me as long as he did not touch my baby sister so this nasty man touch me, I wanted to spit in his face, I hated him and wanted to kill him. Should I tell my adopted mother? She did say she would kill anyone that ever touches me again. or should I tell my real mother what he was doing to me and my little sister? Well I got sick because he touches me again and he felt something move in me and got up off me and said what is that? I told him I was pregnant. So he did not care, I plotted to kill this man and my mother for allowing this to Happen to us, do she really care? What's wrong with her? I hated them both so much, I hated my father for being a drunk and allow his craziness to hurt me, I hated all men even God! but not my brother he was different. So my mother found out that I was pregnant and was mad she called me stupid and a hole, said you probably don't know who the father is? I was okay with the name calling I was use to that with my adopted mother, so I did not care as long as I could stay there to protect my little sister, so my mother went shopping to get me some cloths and baby things, that was the least she could do, I was glad that I was having a baby because someone that I could love and love me back. And maybe my baby will be able to wipe my tears away. I got bigger my brother got out of jail again and found out that I was living with my mother, so he came and got me a lot. He was happy that he was going to be an uncle, he had a son. He was not mad that I was having a baby. I wanted to live with my brother and his girlfriend, she was nice but I was to scare to leave my sister with that man and my mother. So I told my brother about what happen to me and he was mad, he went back to my mothers house and beat up the man and pulled a gun out to kill him and my mother, but I beg him not to, because of my little sister. So my mother called the police and they put my brother back in jail. I hated her for this. My brother said he never ever wanted to see my mother again as long as he live even when he die, he said don't let her come too his funeral.

So as time went by my mother man did not bother me or my sister maybe because he had a Girlfriend on the side, and I was getting bigger, or he was scared when my brother got out of prison he was going to deal with him. I was almost due to have my baby and I threaten him if he touch my sister I was going to kill him in his sleep, and that was a promise! My sister and me would go visit her father at his job some center he worked at he would clean in the evening, and my mother needed someone to watch us, we was old enough to stay home ourselves, but she was doing something she did not want us around the house to see. I had my baby it is a girl, she was very pretty I loved her so much, my sister father tried to mess with me he would offer me money to have sex with him, telling me I look just like my mother and shaped like her too. But I fought back I told him I would cut his stuff off if he ever tried to touch me; I fought back for once in my life. I had something to fight for, my little girl. She gave me a reason to live because if something happen to me the things I went through, I thought she would go through, so I was very protected of her, my mother and her man friend tried to take my baby from me, because he tried to mess with me again, my baby was 3months old and I fought him and beat the mess out of him, I grab a knife and cut him I tried to kill his short behind, and my mother slapped me, and I pushed her down, I did not want to hurt her because of my little sister. My sister was 18 years old. So they called the police on me and tried to take my daughter from me, so I ran, I was going to be eighteen in 1 month family services could not touch me then. So I ran back to my adopted mother house she never asked any questions, just took me in like I was her child and protected me. She was not going to let my mother or anyone else take my baby or me. I was back home! I was still hurting and scared for my sister. But at this time my sister would fight back and run away if she needed to, she was much stronger to defend herself, but after 6 months I heard that man my mother was with, got killed in his driveway I was not sad, I was glad because I hated him and maybe someone killed him for messing with their daughter. I really did not care, as long as my sister was okay. So as time went on my brother wanted me to live with him and his girlfriend she was much older then him I was old enough then. I was eighteen and old enough to live on my own, or go live with my brother, so I decided to go with my brother and his girlfriend, so I can get a job and save so I can be able to live on my own. My brothers girlfriend was very nice, she gave me a roof over my head for me and my daughter and I was free from all the torment I went through in the foster homes

I lived in, I felt this was the best thing God ever done for me. I got a job and was doing pretty good, but still felt a emptiness inside, I had my daughter and sometimes my brother was there but I still did not feel loved, I really did not understand why I was feeling this way, nothing I did or my brother and his friend tried to do, all the friends I met could not wipe my tears away. So time passed and my brother stayed in and out of jail till one time he was gone to long, and I was very angry and upset because he had left me so much and I felt like I would never have a real family. I knew that my brother and my daughter loved me, but it was not enough, I still needed something more, some type of other kind of love that I never knew about that could wipe these tears away, I met a real nice boy he was a singer I was living between my brothers girl friend house and my adopted mother at this time.

I had finished high school, and I knew him there he liked me when we were in school but at that time I did not want to date any boy because of all the things I was going through. but I really did not trust any man at all at this time, I thought about what my grandmother taught me, about saving yourself for the right man, your husband. But I knew that it was to late for me because I was damage goods, so why did this boy like me don't he know that I was damage, so we dated and I met his family he was the only boy and all sisters his mom was nice but crazy, but she did not take any mess, she remind me of my adopted mother very out spoken. Everything that came out her mouth was bad words, she called her kids out their names just like my adopted mother but she loved them and cared for them, I love them and fitted right in, his mother loved me it was nothing she would not do for me. And he was a good man, he never asks to touch me and we dated for six to eight months before we did anything. The day we messed around he said I was going to be his wife I was eighteen and was about to be nineteen years old when he asked me to be his wife. He was the only boy I ever trusted besides my brother. So we moved in with his oldest sister so I could have a home for my daughter, I went with him all the time to hear him sing, then right after my nineteen birthday I was sick, I was pregnant again, so we got married and got our own place I finally had my own family. I really believe that this was love because he was the only man I had to sleep with, and he never force me to do anything I did not want to do, we went months with out having sex, I was glad cause I really hated it, to me it was something nasty and evil, no matter who it was with. And when we did have sex I wanted the lights off and my clothes on, I never wanted to get naked, I felt like God would punish me for exposing my body to anyone, my grandmother would tell me that our bodies was the temple for God to live in. But I knew I had to have sex with him to keep him there so we could be a family. So he started leaving a lot, and things got worst for us and I was about 20 years old and was pregnant again, we argue a lot, because I really did not know how to care for two kids and one on the way, this was not a dream come true, I could not take care of my kids by myself it got hard, I was so scared that I might loose my children because I could not pay rent, he was not working and that was hard on me, so one day I packed all my clothes and left him and went and stayed with my grandmother, so that she could help me since my uncles were not living there any more. I felt safe being there. I thought marring this man and having a family with him that this would wipe my tears and they would go away. I thought that this was real true love the love I never had from anyone, but I guess it was not for me. Maybe every foster parent that told me that I would never be loved, I can't get love, and my life was meaningless, maybe that was why my mother gave us away, maybe that's why my grandmother got sick, maybe that's why no one ever cared about me. Now I am 20 years old and I have three children living with my grandmother, as time went on I worked went back to school and was still feeling like my life was empty, how was this? I have three beautiful children that adore and love me, a grandmother that cared and loved me, she always told me that I was special, and God had a plan for my life that's why I had to go through, she said that I was precious in Gods eyes and he was going to bless me and use me for his Glory, It was to hard to believe that, what do God want to use a damage vessel like me for?

I thought to myself, what is wrong with my grandmother? God don't want me, he hate me he care less what happens to me, and he would never use me with the mess I got in my closet, don't he know that I was not pure any more? And that every man that was a around me took what was precious! So what do I have left to offer God? I am not a virgin any more. So I did what I felt was right for me and my children, I met another guy that was very bad for me, I thought about things that my mother said that between your legs was money so I thought if

I would have sex with him and because he was giving me lots of money to care for my kids I was able to buy them any thing they ever wanted this man would give me the world as long as I sleep with him, and this was a nightmare this guy would beat me all the time, my brother was still locked up and could not protect me I had to fight for my life all the time he wanted me to do things I never ever wanted to do so I would fight back, one day he pulled a gun, put it in my mouth because I was going to leave him, he said that he would kill me and my kids, if I ever would leave him, I tried praying but nothing seemed to work, I was to ashamed to tell my grandmother or adopted mother that this was happening so I decided to kill the man myself. I was going to nursing school and had learn a lot about medicine so I plotted to kill him by giving him something in his food, I hated this man he had tried to strip me from the things I loved that was going to college and my kids, so one night he went to sleep but he had got a call from his sister so he left the house and his sister boyfriend and him got into something and his sister boyfriend shot him and he got killed, that was my ticket of freedom from him, so I decided to relocated to Utah I had some cousins on my father side, lived there and they invited me to come live there, so me and my kids moved, I got back into nursing school, got my kids into church even though I hated it, but I wanted my kids to know that they need to stay with God so that they would not have tears like me that could not be wiped away. I met different men's that liked me but I hated them, because I knew what they all wanted, and that they all were no good, and I was to scare for them to be around my daughter. I did not trust no men so I treated them like I felt, I dated about 2 different men at this time I was about 23 years old. I was in college at this time going to school to become a nurse so I could care for my children and they would not need or want any thing like I did. I was scared that they would go through what I did. I could not ever loose my children, they were all that I had, maybe this was all that I would have from God. So I would only thank him for my children, so he would not allow anything to happen to them. Maybe my mother never thanked him for us, maybe that is why her kids were cursed, she had three kids and I had three kids at the time. As time went by I had met a friend that helped me out a lot she was Spanish and Italian, but just like a real sister. So we hung out all the time. She helped me get a place near her. She was so nice and we hung out all the time, we work, go home and party, I never would drink anything that was strong. I like very light wine or wine coolers; I would drink one here and there never more than two if I were out. One day her brother was giving a party and my friend wanted me to go, but I did not want to because it was a house party and my brother always told me not to go to house parties cause bad things happens at house parties, and they always have drugs there, but she begged and said girl my brothers house is safe and I got your back! Nothing will happen and if you feel funny we will leave, so I trusted her because she had never lied to me and she was my girl.

We shared everything even what was in my past and the things that happened to me. My friend was Spanish and her families were to, all Spanish and Italian, so here we are at this party, it was nice her cousin always liked me, but I did not like him because he was a playboy messed with to many girls for me and he was nasty always looking at me like I was something to eat, just like that one foster parent I had. It was a lot of people there drinking and dancing I loved to dance, I had won lots of dance contests so I danced a lot, I only had one drink because I wanted to stay focus on what was around me. Then her cousin approached me and asked me to dance, so I dance with him and then asked me did I want something to smoke and I told him no I don't smoke and then he asked me did I want something to drink and I told him I don't drink. So then he went and got me a soda so I thought that was okay, he started telling me that I looked sexy and nice and he always wanted to get with me and I told him that I had a man and I was okay. I started looking for my friend because I starting feeling dizzy and my stomach was getting upset but I could not find her some people was talking in Spanish and I got to dizzy I really did not know how I got upstairs but I felt myself falling down on something. And woke up the next day with my clothes off my head was still spinning, but I knew everything that I was seeing, her cousin was putting on his pants, asking me could we see each other later I started crying and could not believe that this had happened again, I did not believe I had just got raped and could not remember the event, what in the world had just happened he approached me and I picked up a lamp and hit him on the head, and starting punching him, I was trying to kill this man, his cousin came in the room to pull me off him, my friends brother, and asked what was going on I told him that his cousin had raped me. they started talking in Spanish and I started running toward the kitchen to get a knife, I was going to kill everyone that was in that house, his cousin was telling me to calm down and lets talk, but I was asking him where was his sister? he said she had went home, I could not believe that she would leave me like this. did they plan this all along? I thought to myself! Why did she allow them to do this to me? I screamed inside because I had let her know about something's that had happened to me in my past. was she really a friend? or did God tell her to pretend she like me so I could be curse again. Her brother talked to me and took me home saying that he was so sorry for what had happened and he did not know that his cousin had put some type of date rape drug in my soda. But I did not care what he was saying because I was mad inside and was blocking out everything he was saying. When I got home all I could think of is getting even with my so-called friend. I did not care about what I was going to face because I was mad beyond measure, and I could care less about what anyone was going to say. I was to mad at the world again. And now these tears were coming back to haunt me. My friend tried to call me but I would not return any of her calls, I was hurt because I believed that she had set me up. After a while I shook it off because I felt like it was my fault I should of not went their knowing that men were there, and my body did not belong to me. I was curse to men forever, and I thought that they could take it anytime God said they could, it was that name of the game for me. My relationship will never be the same with any man. How could I explain that I got raped? I was dressing to sexy for one, and was going out a lot with my friend, no one would believe me any way, so why bothered.

After a while I was getting sick it was about three to fours months later after the raped had happened, so I went to the doctor to make sure that everything was okay, I could of caught something from my friends cousin, I wanted to make sure that I was okay, and boy was I surprise, I was pregnant what a shocker, I was so blown away I knew it was to good to be true living here in Utah. Kill me Lord and take me out of my misery, did God make me so that the men would have sex with me? I believe if I did die they would even take it when I am dead, so maybe God should just burn me up. So I put a wall of a hard heart toward all men. I wonder what was I going to do no one could find out, should I get an abortion or what? I thought to myself. But God said Thy should not kill any innocent child, and I had not talked to my girlfriend in three to four months. What would I do so I called her up, and she was so happy to here from me and the first thing she said to me was that her cousin was asking about me and he liked me. What a joke I said because how could someone like me and rape me at the same time? She said girl I know, and he is sorry for what he did. He was drunk and wanted you so bad, he thought that would be the only way he could get with you. I told her I really don't care about how he feels because he messed up my life I was pregnant by him, she was happy, for what! I wondered, she said maybe you and him can get together now, I started thinking that my girlfriend was crazy, who want to be with some one who raped them? Who want to be with a scum like him? I hated him. So she asked me what was I going to do? I don't know so we talked every day to figure out a plan we told him and he wanted me to have the baby and he would take care of the child, and that was out of the question, because if he did this to me he might do it to my daughter, and I really did not know him or trust him, so we came up with a plan that I would send my kids home for a little while and have the baby, and she would raise the child. So I decided to do just that. I had a favorite aunt that I loved so much, she was so nice and helped my grandmother with me when I stayed with my grandmother, I use to think that she was my mother for a minute, because she cared for me just like a mother should, but she was just my aunt she was to young to be my mother. So I planned to send my kids back east to my Auntie I love. She decided to help care for my kids while I was in Utah, and I told her I would pay her and she told me that she would do what she can, and don't worry the kids would be okay. She kept the kids for a while for me I had 5 months to go to have the baby and I needed that much time so no one would know. It was so confusing to make a decision, I was getting close to this child it seemed like she would grab me and hold me from the inside. And the guy that raped me wanted to be in her life and mine. But I hated him and was scared that I would hate my child to, and I never had a child from another race, and that was scary to deal with. My friend she went to every doctor appointments with me and she was getting attached and we found out the baby was a girl. And I used her name every time I went to the doctors because I did not want to take the chance of my children and family looking at me different, and not loving me since they were the only ones that truly loved me and never hurt me. So I had her and she was beautiful, I named her after my god daughter I had back east and I gave her to my friend after I got out the hospital we had her name on the birth certificate because I used her name when I went into the hospital, so that she would be able to raise her with out any problems and care for her.

My baby girl was three weeks when I departed from her life. I never gave any of my children up no matter what. It was so hard the worst thing I ever had to go or do It was the worst than my past and rapes, I never felt something so painful in my life, I cried and cried and cried for many days and many nights. But my friend and me did decide that I would be in her life and I would be her Godmother. And she would keep the child because I really did not want a child that people would wonder about, but for some reason this child was feeling special to me. Even through my friend and me had decided that I would have the baby and pretend that the child was hers and she promised me that she would not let anything ever happen to her, like what happen to me. I felt that it would be the best thing for all of us not to explain that I had another child from being raped. My first daughter was from a relation that was not planned, so I was sacred to let anyone know the truth at this time. So I went back to Ohio it was 1980 to be with my other children and I had heard that my brother had been released From prison and was looking for me so I had stayed back in Ohio for 5 years I called to check on my baby girl all the time. And my children were happy to see me, I wanted to tell them so bad that they had a baby sister, but I was so ashamed of what I did, and was scared of loosing their love. And I had enough problems just being me, I did tell my Aunt and my brother and they supported me. Having a mix child would have been difficult so people could throw more stones at me. And I thought that men would really attack me seeing that I had kids all different colors they would think I would mess with every man on the planet. And I felt like my baby would be with me all the holidays and birthdays and summers and we would be very close and the kids would know that they were her brothers and sister. I am back in Ohio and I met a nice guy and his uncle gave me a house so we moved in together, he knew every thing even about my daughter in Utah and never judge me just told me that we will get her back one day, and everything was going fine. That was too hard to believe from anyone. My brother had came home again from prison and I wanted to go see my real mother so she could know that I had children her grandchildren. So I asked my brother again and he said yes this time I was so happy, so that weekend was a holiday, fourth of July he decided to take me to New York I was 22 years old and the year was 1981. We started our journey to New York to see my mother me my brother and his lady friend, we did not know where we was going but we got there I was so sacred because my brother still did not like our mother and I was scared of what he would say to her I just wanted us to have a good visit and she would say that she was sorry for what she have done to us and I could tell her about what everyone have done do me and to let her know that I had four children. As we drove through the state of New York it was crazy we seen all types of people, prostitutes, people on drugs it was crazy since they said my mother was a prostitutes so maybe we might see her on the streets. But we found the house someone back home gave us where she lived and we pulled up to the house. And I got out and knocked on the door and a man came to the door and asked me what did I want?

And I said we were looking for our mother and he asked who is your mother? And I said her name and he said she lives here, but she doesn't have any kids but one child. And I ask him could she come to the door so we can ask her because the name were the same, and our family told us that our mother lived here. After asking a few times he decided to call her to the door only because he said I look like her so I must be some kin, my stomach started to hurt as he called her to the door, I was scared that she might be another woman, because why don't he know all about her other children? My brother at this time got out the car so that he could hear what was being said, he did not want to see her but wanted to make sure I was okay. She appeared at the door and my eyes were shock because it was her woman that I had lived with. She said what do you kids want? Like she did not even know us! And I said we came to see you and our little sister. And our mother said what little sister? I have only one child, and she is not your sister. I said what? What are you talking about, I said because you are my mother, she said I am not your mother honey, at this time my brother got real upset because we had came so far and this lady was denying that she was our mother. I was so hurt I could not believe she would ever say something like this, she asked us to leave but her male friend wanted to know why we were calling her our mother, so he asked her. And she told him she did not know we were her sister kids and she help raised us so we might think she was our mother. My eyes were full of tears and because I was crying, my brother walked up from his car and was getting real upset because he promised me that no one would ever make me shed a tear again, as long as he was around me and living, so he started telling my mother what he really thought about her and was saying some really bad things, cursing at her, it looked like he was about to hit her, I just wanted them to stop urging, then my mothers male friend came out the door with a big shoot gun telling us to get away from his house, my brother was not afraid he had walked toward the gun and told him that he had nothing to do with it our mother was a liar, and we were her kids that she left us to die in a house and do what he want to do shoot because we came to far to let a no good mother like her deny her blood, so shoot me if you think that would solve her mess, but he was going to speak his mind. I started screaming begging my mother to tell the truth so that my brother would not get hurt, but she pushed me away and said that she was going to call the police, so I begged my brother to leave so that he would not get in trouble and he would not go to jail, then his lady friend got out the car and told my brother to get in the car because he could get into trouble. My brother was on parole in Ohio and if they knew that he was in New York he would go back to prison. We only had 20 dollars to our name to get back on, what a hot mess. And we never got to see our little sister at all I really did not know where she were, if she was in the house or did she get rid of her. I cried all the way back home. I believe my brother now that our mother was no good, she never cared about us and never would, to allow a man to pull a gun on her own son was terrible what kind of mother would let someone take a life of her child? It was a nightmare going to New York, I told my brother that I was sorry and I would never bring her name up again and I was so thankful that God did not allow this man to hurt my brother.

When I got home I told my man friend what my mother had done. It was so hard to put all that behind us. And my brother told me to promise him that if anything ever happened to him that I would not allow that woman to come to his funeral. I still did not like my brother talking like he was going to die but I promise him that I would not allow her to come because he would not stop talking about it. After time it was about 2 months later my brother ended back in prison they had given him 3 years for violating his probation, and this was hard, but my life went on, me and the man stayed together for a long time and we both had good jobs and nothing bad was happening but I still felt empty and alone with him and my children for a while I was not able to get in touch with my best friend in Utah I was getting a little worried about that, but I worked and took care of home and my friend did to, the 3 years went by fast for my brother to be coming home from prison and he had got paroled to my house, I was so glad we had a lot to talk about, my brother was living with me and another lady friend off and on and every day he was bothering me about getting insurance on him that something might happen to him, my brother always wanting to take care of me no matter where he was, and he did not care a lot about my male friend, Maybe because he thought that he could not protect me, if something happened to him, my brother did not feel anyone was good enough for his sister, so why did I feel that this man could not wipe all my tears away? Knowing that my brother loved me more than anyone, even God, me and my brother caught up on every thing he missed in my life, my brother was so full of life and never let nothing or no one stand in his way, at this time I was talking to my brother about forgiving our mother but he still hated her, I had some nerve when I hated all the people that ever hurt me. And believe me he would get mad at me for even wanting to say her name, but I never gave up on talking to him about her no matter what he said. So time went on and we made the best of living our life the best way we knew how. As time went on my brother would talk to me about getting life insurance on him over and over again, I would get mad and tell him to stop talking foolish, but he continue saying the same thing over and over I asked him what are you planning to do kill yourself? I told him don't try, because God would not allow that because I tried to many times to end my life and God would not let me die he wanted us to suffer because we were cursed from having a mother like we did, and her sins infected us from living a normal life, this is what most of the foster homes I lived in told me, my brother told me no, I just want you to be taking care if something ever happen to me. That's why he wanted me to do this. Now it is October of 1985 and this is when my life changed every thing that I lived for was really hitting me in the face I could feel everything that ever happened to me come back alive. I was at work working midnights and a phone call came to my job saying that my brother just got shoot! I ran from my job jumped in my car and droved straight to the place where my brother was laying in the streets, with my tears over flowing I jumped out the car and ran toward my brother, I was there before the police and ambulance. Holding my brother in my arms with his head on my lap trying to stop the bleeding and telling him to hold on, saying please don't leave me.

My brother was trying to talk but I would not let him, telling him to just hold on I looked up toward a place they say heaven asking God to please don't let my brother die, this is all I have, I know lord that you care less about me and you never answered none of my prayers ever, but would you please have mercy on me and spare my brothers life? My brother was calling my name so I looked down at him and he had one tear coming down his face telling me I love you baby girl, take care of the little soldiers, and he took his last breathe and closed his eyes, as I wiped the tear from my brother eye. I felt nothing, my body was numb I don't even know how I made it home! I was in shock for days I never wanted to talk to God ever again, how did my grandmother worship this God! did she know how he was treating her grandchild? I really did not want to let go of my brother no matter what people said or done, I just wanted to be left alone. Even through my friends I had try to help me deal with this even the man I was with, him and my brother had the same name. But I hated life and every one around me but my babies, I held them every night close to me, they tried to wipe my tears away but nothing they did work. Now it is time to prepare my brother funeral, I had to sell things in my house, and people gave money because my brother had no life insurance, I never did what he ask me to do, maybe he knew that he was going to die, maybe God told him that he was going to die? My mother ha what a laugh came down I really did not want her here, why would she come when she said that we were not her kids? Why did she care? My grandmother always told me to forgive people no matter what they do or say to you. But I did not want to forgive her. I blamed her for my brother getting killed and my brother did not want her here. And I promised him that I would not allow her to come. Maybe the quilt killed her, she should have been ashamed to even showed her face, I said to myself. I had all types of emotion going on inside, I felt like Sybil, with all types of personalities some time I was up and sometimes I was down. I had wondered how my mother knew that my brother had got killed after she had told her man friend that we were not her children, how did she tell him that she had to come and buried a son after she had told him she only had one child, but I found out that my Grandmother had called to New York and told the man that we were her children, now her husband knew the truth, so how do she feel because her little secret was out, the box! The man knew that we were telling the truth we were her children, I wonder how did she deal with that mess? But honestly I did not even care. I was so stress out and everybody getting on my nerves like they really cared, where was every one when we were going through hell? My mother acted like she had raised my brother all his life with her sad cry. I truly wanted to go with my brother, I asked God so many nights to take me with my brother, but when I looked at my kids I said how could I leave them with these messed up people in this world. No one would take care of them or make sure nothing happened to them. Then I thought about the man I was living with maybe he would care for them, we have been together a long time and he has not tried to mess with my daughter or anything, he loved them like they were his own, he would be the best person I could leave them with, but I was scared that they would never get to meet their baby sister so I got to stay around to find her for them, and I don't want them to feel this pain I feel of loosing a love one.

But I just could not trust it so I guess I was stuck in this crazy messed up world, maybe God gave me children so I could stay here longer to suffer. Maybe I would take all our life's, but I remember thy shall not kill, my grandmother told me especially innocent children, but I wanted to kill my mother, father, uncle, and all them foster home parents, especially the guy that took my brother away. Everyone that allowed things to happen to me, they were not innocent by no means. But times got so hard for me to deal with, I did not want to go to work, go outside or out my room. I had not call to Utah to see how my baby girl was doing, and I have not heard from my friend either. Since my brother got killed, it has been six months, I was not doing good at all so we decided to move back to Utah I went first to get things together for my family and a cousin had invited me to stay with him and wife so I could get my life back in order and better myself there, and he and his wife would help me out, so I decided to move to Utah so I could finish Nursing school I had 1 and half year to go. My male friend wanted to go but he had a job and was coming up later after I find a place for us to stay, so I went while him and the kids stayed just for three months. I Was in Utah for 30 days got a job and a place to live because I had to work fast while I was staying with my cousin and his wife I was very uncomfortable his wife was very nice, but he was nuts he looked at me all the time when I walked, he made me feel so uncomfortable, and wanted to hug to much and then one night he tried to have sex with me, I pulled a knife on him and he told me to get out his house, his wife was scared of him, but she believed me. And tried to help me, so she gave me money to get a motel room for a week I was so mad and upset. Here I was again, that I would come over two thousand miles from Ohio and the same plague in my family has followed me again! I guess I was cursed and nothing and nowhere would make a difference at all. I worked hard to get my place I had a nice job and met some good friends that helped me out better then people in Ohio. I was doing so good and things looked great until my own blood relations started making sexually movements on me. I really thought that God would not allow this to keep going on; maybe it was out of his control! I started thinking that I had a tattoo on me that only the world could see and not me saying body for any one to touch, I hated my body, I looked at it like it was nothing but evil. I wanted God to allow me to rest and never wake up but I thought relocate back to Utah with my best friend and baby girl maybe this would help some of my tears. Maybe a change of scenery would help me; it was hard to be in Ohio where my brother lost his life. So this is why I decided to move back to Utah and I told the kids that they had a new sister. God sister that is, but I got a surprise of my life my friend had moved back to Puerto Rico, her whole family went back and left me no address nothing I never knew that this was going down. She never told me that they were leaving, I could not believe this I could not find my daughter at all, who could I tell? When no one knew that I had another child but my deceased brother and aunt back in Ohio, I went in the hospital using her name all my doctor appointments were in her name I used her insurance so what could I do I was messed up. But I was not going to give up no matter what to find her.

I found a place that was so nice and my male friend and children came up he had got a job on the Air Force Base,

I was to ashamed to ask for help, I knew God was punishing me for doing what I done in the first place. So as time went on the kids would ask, when were they going to see their god sister? And I told them soon she lives out of town. So time went on they was happy being back with me and I was mad, hurt, let down, betrayed, I felt so stupid this was the second time this family hurt me I was out for blood. I knew I had lost my daughter forever, I wanted to pray but I knew that God would not hear me or would laugh at me and say that this is what you get. Why tell my family because I had no family that really cared. So why complain, so we lived in Utah for 4 years and my tears got heavier and heavier and I started feeling no matter where I lived God hated me no matter what I do God hated me, no matter what I said God hated me. Then one summer I moved in a different neighborhood and one day I was riding down the street and seen a car that looked like my friends old car, I wanted to stop but I was running late for work, but as I droved off I could not stop thinking about that car. It was like a voice was talking to me all that morning at work, So on my lunch break I went home the car was gone. Then the next day I droved down the street and that same car was there so I stopped! A little girl came to the door looking like a light skin Minnie me. Tears were in my eyes, and I was shaking, I could not believe what I just seen she looked like she was about seven or eight and I asked her what was her name and she told me. At this time someone came from the back room, and it was my friend she ran and hugged me and said I know, I know how you feel. She cannot imagine how I felt I was to happy to be mad, to happy to be sad and go off because my baby girl was looking so good she had took good care of her and she seemed like she had everything that she ever wanted. My friend and me played caught up and she told me that her so-called dad did a lot for her and he was still In Puerto Rico and that he had part custody with her concerning my daughter I could not really say a lot concerning that since I gave up rights by using her name as the mother, but I thank her for keeping me involved in her life and letting me know about every thing so we became close again, My baby girl was back in my life, and she got to finally meet her sister and brothers even though we told them that she was their god sister, but they had a closeness that you would have with your real family, you could not tell that they were not family they act like they never were apart. I would ask myself all the time why did God make me a pincushion? This was my second time living in Utah the first time my kids were only little babies their ages were four two and one and this is when I left there father because he was not trying to do anything in his life at that time, and I wanted more for my family and I wanted to better myself and do better by my children, better then my parents were with me. When I lost my brother I just could not face life at that time. If I would not have moved back to Utah I would of never found my baby girl. So maybe the Lord said he would do one nice thing for me after all. I wanted to thank him but my heart was to numb and heavy to open my mouth to say the words. He had brought my family together, I never had anything to be thankful for only my children, and I thank him for that. So as time went on I started messing up the relationship with the man I was with, I did not know how to love, I did not believe in love, and I was scared to even receive love, because I thought it would be only a joke played on me! so I kept my heart hard.

My baby girl had breathing problems like me I had asthma and she did to, just like my oldest daughter we were so much alike, and the boys were ok they never had any problems with their lungs. As time went on I never said a word to my children because I just was to scared to loose their respect or love, I felt like I was just like my mother and was doing and going to do what she did to me and my brother and the way I felt about her and my father I did not want my kids to feels that same pain but I believe in my heart that they knew that she was their real sister. So I kept this secret but I did tell the man I was with the truth so that he would tell if I would ever die I felt that God would not let me live to long for all that I have done in my past. Or maybe God did not know what I did because he never expose the truth, knowing that he had all the cards to my life he always dealt me a bad hand no matter how much I tried to prove myself to him, he would hurt me, the Lord hated me. Because it cost me my brother, but I just wanted my children to be happy, and my kids loved it in Utah, my male friend and me had good jobs. We were doing well. But still I was hurting for something that was still missing in my life. What is it I wonder to myself? I have a nice home, a nice car, a good job, good friends, a good man, awesome children, and nice cloths and shoes, I had enough stuff to give to 20 families. I had love from lots of people now that I never knew that could love someone like me, so what was missing out of my life? So I hid everything that ever happened to me inside, I cried off and on, no one could understand what was going on with me, I was an emotional roller coaster. Even though I had a good man at home I wanted more maybe that was what it was so I dated other men even though I did not care much for them I just wanted to use them I wanted to hurt every man the way I was hurt. So I only use them for what I could get out of them but that still did not fill the emptiness that was stabbing me in the heart. Because every man I came into contact with always wanted sex for love, it was always drop the pants or pull up your skirt, what do this got to do with love? Even sex did not wipe my tears away. I was so closed up inside full of hurt, shame and pain. I felt that this was a way of life for everyone maybe other people went through the same thing I went through and just kept it inside, maybe they moved to new places so no one could identify them. It was nice to be somewhere where other people did not know what happened to you, so I separate myself from family and made up family as I met new people, I did not like my real family at all I thought they had some type of disease that allowed them to act the way they did and I did not want my children to inherit that disease, so I kept them away. I stayed in Utah for 8 more years and my baby sister had got older and had got in touch with me what a good thing because I sent for her to come and live with us in Utah she had a male friend and I did not care I wanted her with me so we could wipe each others tears away, but when she came I was disappointed she came with a house full her man his brother and his lady friend I did not know these men and did not trust them around my girls at all, they looked rough and my sister did too at this time I just wanted to help her, We talked laugh and cried together she had told me all kinds of things that had happened to her I hated the mother we called mom for how she raised my sister rough, my sister never had a good normal life a life of drugs, prostitution, sex, and crime, what a life to have as a childhood.

No wonder she had a choice of bad men in her life my heart hurt for her, but after a while I could not keep them their because of all the fighting that was going on between them and the other couple and my friend said they had to go so after a real bad fight one night I had to let them go, but me and my baby sister stayed in touch no matter what. Her life was full of in and out of prisons just like my brother. I was upset with my man friend because I hated to choose to send my sister away because she got into trouble and I was not able to help wipe her tears away. So we had problems one after another but he still was excellent to my children, and we shared a secret Together concerning my baby girl, as time went on it was 1990 I started to get sick and I stayed sick all the time, I could not understand what was going on so I went to the doctors and took all kinds of test I was not pregnant and that was good, but something worst was going on they told me that I had cancer I just could not believe my ears what a trauma, I can't have this no I said to myself why is everything always happening to me!

Doesn't God have someone else to pick on? I can't have cancer who is going to care for my children who? I started really not liking this God but still was to scared to stop my kids from serving him, because he took care of them nothing happened to them like it happened to me, so I kept them in church more and more, I talked to my best friend about my sickness and she was crying with me and she told me about a hospital that helped her aunt but the hospital was in New York I have not thought of that place no more since my brother died that was the place my Real mother lived what was God trying to do to me, I really wanted to go to New York so I could get well and get rid of this cancer so that I could live and care for my children myself, so as time went by I got sicker and weaker and could not care for myself a lot I stayed in bed, and my Grandmother called and told my mother that she need to help me. Because she never had done anything ever in my life, so she did contact me and told me that Rochester had the best cancer hospital and she wanted me to come there. She came down met my male friend and her grandchildren again the last time she meet them was in 1985 when my brother Curtis had past away. And she helped me drove back east because I was to week to drive, my male friend stayed because we had to much stuff and he had to wait to come later so he could get things together, we talked a little on the way to New York not much, I really did not have much to say I was to mad at God to even had put me in this situation. We arrive at the hospital in New York it was very big I really did not want to stay because I had to let my mother care for my children, I did not trust her at any means necessary, but what choice did I have. But I did threaten her and let her know that nothing better not happen to my kids while their were in her cared or I would blow New York up with her and her husband in it. She looked at me like I was crazy, and I said to myself I am crazy when it comes to my children my baby girl was back in Utah with my friend I could not bring her because of the arrangements I had made in the past and no one knew she was my biological child. So I wrote a will incase anything happened to me in the hospital I wanted my kids to go back with my male friend or my auntie in Ohio and I wanted my children to know that their god sister was their real sister, I was to much of a coward to tell them when I was alive. I just could not lose their respect or love.

I missed her and so did her sister and brothers, but they were busy meeting new friends and I was in the hospital getting well it had been six months I was going for chemo and radiation treatment my male friend had drove up and got a place for us that was good because I did not want to be around a woman that really did not love me, and I thought that the reason why she stepped in to help is that if I die she would get my kids and money and everything I ever owned. After being there eight month the doctors could not find any kind of cancer in my body like it was never there, they ran all kinds of test over and over again and nothing, what a joke everyone told me that it was God and my grandmother said that it was one of God miracles, I did not believe that because I knew that God hated me so why would he heal someone like me? Nevertheless I stayed in New York I got a job at the hospital and my man friend was working, even through I was cured from cancer I still felt that I was dead inside something was eating inside of me I still did not feel the love I needed to wipe my tears away. I was in a very rebellious state of mind, I did not care or love anyone but my children so I completely mess up my relationship with my man friend I was with for thirteen years, the love he was trying to give me was not enough to heal me from the pain that had me shed tears, I was tired of living with him sleeping with him or looking at him I never wanted to marry him because I was still married to my sons father we never divorced, the relationship I had built with my mother was not good enough because all we did was argued because she felt that she never done anything wrong living her life as a one big lie after another. At this time I had heard that my father was sick living with my aunt in Detroit I had not forgiven my father for what he had done to me, even though he was in my life off and on, when I was living in Ohio he knew my children better than my mom because he tried to make up with me over and over again, it was that my pain was so deep it was to hard to let him in. my father was still drinking and I was scared to let him to close to me so I monitor him with my children when he was in their life, it was so funny because my father was so good with my children and they loved their grandfather I never told them any thing bad about him, I wanted them to have a relationship with him in spite of what he did to me. I loved my father because he really had tried to be a good father. He tried to buy me everything I ever wanted. But it never made up enough to wipe my tears away. I got a call that my father had died January 1991, I cried it really hurt that I was not able to forgive him I really loved my father and it was to late to let him know that, I went to the funeral me and my man friend and when I actually seen him laying in the casket I broke it hurt so much to see him laying there I beg him to forgive me for not forgiving him I told him that I loved him even though he did not hear me I really felt that he heard me I cried out loud and said daddy I love you forgive me for how I ever treated you! I just never had told him that because my hurt and pain would not let me forgive him. While I was at my father funeral, I meet a sister and brother that my father had while he was living in Chicago there were younger than me we talked a little I really did not know them at all, I never knew that my father had other children, I was to hurt to really cared all I knew is that I was his only child. But I always wanted a family.

After the funeral I went back to New York my mother act like she did not care that my father even die she would tell me I never want to hear that name in my house, that because she had lied to her husband about my father he never knew that she was married to my father before, he only knew about my sister father. She was a hot mess because I was proud of my father no matter what he had ever done I only wanted to remember that he really loved me. He was a professional boxer but his drinking destroyed his life. After a while things got bad in my relationship and I did not want to be with my man friend, So we split up, at this time I did not care about my life I thought if I would be happy it was a sin, or something and God would punish me for it, so why try. I could not stand my mothers husband he was very sneaky, every time he see me he looked just like the foster parents men look at me like I was something to eat, I did not like the way he touched me or talk to me my mother was in such a denial concerning him that man was no good and up to no good. But he never tried to mess with me he knew I would cut him up in sizes, I had always asked my daughter did he ever tried to touch her or make her feel uncomfortable and she said no, so he was lucky. So I moved back to Ohio and started back with the life I had, Now it is September 1991 my baby brother had lost his life, just a baby I just could not receive this another brother I had to see leave my life, I loved my baby brother so much no one would of thought I was his adopted sister we were so close and his smile had always light up a room he had got killed from a gun shot just like my older brother, I really could not deal with the bad news it was so bad that other young men died with him, how much more pain will I shed tears about? I never knew that a person could shed that much tears, It is 1994 my Adopted mother was very ill she had cancer, I really did not want to move away but all the bad memories, here in Ohio but I had to stay after all she had done for me, she had saved me from all the monster in that place, I wished she would of known about all the monster's all over because she would if made sure that I was protected, I hated to go back to a place where nothing but punishment was at. But if I had to go through anything then it will not matter because what could get worst then what I have already been through? So I packed up my children and moved back to Ohio we had stayed with my Adopted mom for awhile but it was very crowed their so I moved in my own place, and things were getting rough at this time I had applied for disability because of the illness I had earlier and was waiting on that to come through so times were rough like always in this place, I was going to the club sometimes with family members and meeting all the wrong people but I really did not care at the time it was six months later and I still had not received any income and I was loosing my home so a guy that I was dating asked me to move in with him at this time I was going to church with a foster sister of mine and they taught us that we do not live with men unless we are married to them or the wrath of God would come down on us, so it was killing me to do this and I hated it because I never wanted to live with this guy, he was not my kind of man at all but he gave us a roof over my head and food on the table for me and my kids, none of my family helped me out so this is what I had better than being homeless.

As time, went on my adopted mother seem to be doing good for someone that had lung cancer, and my life was fading in front of me this man did everything I hated in a man sex, drugs, he was a male prostitute and I was dealing with trying to live for God for once in my life, I decided to give my life to God I heard one day that if you be born again you would be a new creature, and that stuck with me and I wanted to be born again so I could have a new identity then maybe God would bless me like he did the people in the church. But it was hard I was living in sin fornicating with the man I was living with, how could I live a new life when I got to have sex with this man so my kids could have a roof over their head. I tried praying to God to see if he would bless me with a place of my own but it seemed like that did not work at all. So times got worse and things got touch, I went to church one night and the preacher was preaching about if you live in sin you would go to hell and I was scared that I had my kids living in sin and I did not want them to go to hell and then I heard the message concerning a family in the bible how what he did cursed his children and I felt like that was what my mother had did to me and my brother cursed our life so I decided to take my own life so that my kids would not suffer my mistakes like my mother did me. Then I heard a message that if you do not forgive then God would not forgive you and I could not forgive my mother or my father or my uncles nor my foster parents or my baby girl father why should I they do not deserve my forgiveness they had messed up my life, this is why I am like I am I wanted to be a virgin until I got married I wanted to be married before I had any children, I only wanted one man in my life, I wanted to obey the ten commandments but how could I? They made it impossible for me to do this. Life was not fair at all for me I was domed. I could not take it any more, the man I was with was a dog he slept with everyone that he could had a baby on the way and it seemed like God would not bless me to move for nothing in the world it was not what I wanted for my children. The house was not what we was use to living in, and I hated this for my kids it looked like all the foster homes I lived in a hot mess, drinking, cursing, just a wild life I had took out a nice insurance policy on my self and asked the man that had helped me raise my kids that I was with for 13 years would he raise them if anything ever happened to me and he said he would, we talk all the time because we were still good friends. So it was New Years Eve I thought about taking my life so that my kids would have a good life with the large insurance policy I had, they would be well off and get out this rat whole of a place, but when I tried I was reading they policy and writing my kids a letter and trying to take the pills but what ever it had made me sick and my asthma kicked in the large pill got stuck in my throat and I could not get it out it had blocked my lung where I could not breathe at all no one was around to help me. I was praying that no would think I tried to commit suicide because the insurance policy would not pay. So I was not trying to kill myself I wanted to but it would have been worst for my children, I was trying to take my asthma pill when it got stuck down the wrong pipe and the next thing I knew I was in a coma and woke up march 12 1995 three months had went by and I never knew I was in a coma but I heard voices through it all, I knew that people were talking to me, and I could not answer them, I had lost oxygen to my brain for over 12 hours before anyone had found me lying on the couch Un caution on top of my 2-year-old granddaughter my older daughter had a baby girl that I loved dearly. The whole time I was in the coma my deceased brother was talking to me I could see him and hear him telling me to go back I could not come with him my children need me and I got a great life ahead of me, he kept saying that I had life's depending on me, that God was going to use me! And then he said follow me toward the light and I followed him he gave me a hug and told me that he loved me and he was with me and will be with me. And then I woke up from being in the coma, it was three months later every nurse and doctors came in and called me a miracle child they had already had diagnosed me as being brain dead or a vegetable and told my children and family to prepare to buried me. I was living on life support from three months. I had remembered almost everything my kids my name half my family and everything that I had owned. What did God want with me? Was he saving me every time I try to die? What is my purpose here on earth? What do he have in me that need to live? I had so many questions in my head for God. Everyone was so happy to see me awoke I had got all types of visits from people I never knew church People, business people, professional people, why do people care? I asked myself over and over again. As time went by it seemed like nothing ever had happen I was walking and talking and doing the things I use to do, everyone was shock to see how I recovered so soon, when the doctor's said that I would not make it through and if I had I would be brain dead I was in a coma for three months and came home in a wheel chair but was walking by the time my oldest daughter graduated. It was within three months and I was back to my routine again. Every church person I talked with said God got something great for you to do, his angel was protecting me and his grace and mercy was over my life, I thought about that and I wanted to believe that but it was to hard to receive, thinking about what had happened in my past. I lost contact with my best friend in Utah concerning my baby girl; did she think I forgot all about her? Did she know that I was in a coma? All contact numbers were different and I was sad that I was not able to know how she was doing. At this time I was going to church but was not saved. I was going because a man friend of my brother had invited me, he had told me that my brother had told him to look after me, my brother it was hard to believe because my brother was not a church boy so how did he hang with this guy but I found out later that my brother was friends with his brother and they knew each other, so I starting going to church with him I was still living with the guy I was with before I was in a coma, I remembered this day good this day changed my life it was my birthday September 1995 I walked in the church the doors seemed to open all by themselves, I felt like I was someone very important because everyone came up to me and shock my hand they seemed to be very nice, then the pastor and his wife came up and his wife gave me a big hug and said in my ear God told me that you would be coming soon, I looked surprise because I did not know her but she seemed to know me and she told me her and her husband had came to visit me in the hospital, and had prayed for me every day and knew God had to much work for me to do.

I felt very welcome the songs and testimonies and the preaching word was awesome, as I sat in my seat I kept hearing a soft voice talking to me, I thought it was my friend talking to me, but when I looked at him his mouth was not moving he was praising God, then I heard the voice again saying come to me and I will give you rest and wipe them tears away! And love you like no other can, the voice was so strong that it moved my whole body. I never felt this way before I jumped up and my legs started trembling and I started to shake and tears were flowing down my face, like a river. I could not stop myself the closer I got to the alter I started feeling lighter and lighter, I felt like I never felt before I could not understand what was happening all I knew is that it felt good, a feeling I never felt in my life. I finally was at the alter and the pastor came to me and asked me did I want to be save? Give my life to Jesus? I did not understand, I thought he wanted me to hang on the cross like Jesus did for us he gave his life for us so I thought I had to do the same thing, so the pastor explained what being save meant, by letting me know that I had to be Godly sorry for all my sins, and ask God to forgive me for all the sins I have done, except God to come in my heart, allow the lord spirit to live in me, believe in my heart that Jesus died for my sins, be baptize in Jesus name so that I could be cleanse with the blood of Jesus, and allow the lord to renew my mind by reading his word daily, believe that Jesus is my lord and savior, I could not stop the tears from coming down my face it was like we needed a bucket, all I ever wanted was God to love me and wipe my tears away and have good a life. So I screamed yes I had excepted what the pastor was saying, I did not understand why I had to repent and say I was sorry for anything or to ask for forgiveness, because I felt everything I have done up to this point was not my fault, and why the people that made me this way why they did not have to repent and ask for forgiveness? But at that moment a voice let me know that the things that happen had to happen for a great purpose in my life and I would understand as I walk with him daily I was so shock that God was really talking to me, the first time ever I heard his voice speaking to me. And answering my questions. Maybe the lord do care for me, what have I done to deserve this I wondered? I screamed loud saying Lord please forgive me please save me I am so tired lord of living the way I have been living, lord I am tired of feeling the pain and sorrow I have been feeling lord I am tired please come into my life and fix it lord make me a new person lord, a better person lord please forgive me for all my sins and forgive the ones that sinned against me, I forgive them lord please forgive me make me over I want to be born again. Lord wipe all the tears that I have shed and still coming, I want a change lord I believe you died on the cross for me, lord help me please help me I surrender my all to you I cast every heavy load I got and every tear I shed at your feet. I realize at that moment I was truly tired of being tired of the way I was living I felled to my knees on the floor at the alter, at that moment I received feeling that had took control of me I started shouting the name of the lord my mouth was moving and I had no control of it my body was feeling great I was feeling like I never felt before I felt so good I never wanted to stop.

I felt the heaviness of my heart being lifted off of me and my tears were not tears of sorrow or pain but joy and happiness, I danced all over that church no one could hold me it was to powerful. They could not baptize me until the following Sunday because I praised the lord all that day. When I got home things felt different I looked at myself for the very first time in a mirror and saw nothing but beauty, I was looking good, I looked like a bright shinning star I did not see that little girl that was ugly, scared, unwanted, abandon, rejected, abused or ashamed. I wanted to live, and start living this new life I was giving again. I had read in the bible that you can cast all you cares and all your past sins on God and he would cast it in the sea of forgetfulness and you can start over and your tomorrow is brand new. So it was time to make some changes in my new life, I could not live with this guy I was living with, but I had no money still waiting on my disability to come, so I also read in the bible that if your life be pleasing to God you can ask what you need and God would supply all your needs according to his riches and glory, and I need to please God so my life could be pleasing in his eyes, I really did not know how to pray and I heard my friend say just talk to God like you would your man friend or kids or just talk to him like he was your best friend, so I got in a secret place of the house and purred out my heart out to God and told him what I needed to be able to start living right for him, and boy didn't prayer work they next two days my disabilities check came before the approval letter, it was enough to get a house , buy furniture, a car, and food for me and my kids, I moved in 12 hours thanking God for all he was doing for me I never took care of myself by myself it was always someone I had to depend on like a man but God was my new man now and I did not haven't to sleep with the lord to be bless all he ever wanted from me was a relationship, as I was reading my bible daily and going to church I found out that God was a jealous God and would not have any other Gods before him. The way I were feeling lately it was like I was born for the very first time. It felt like I was loved for the very first time in my life, every thing was going great I loved waking up starting my day, going to church and praising God, I still wanted to know why I had to forgive those who really cared less about me, so I was learning about having a hard heart, bible study was on having a clean heart it seemed like every time I would enter into the house of God It was teaching me something new I thought that I was okay because I gave my life and excepted Christ in my life, but I never knew I had to learn how to over come the past that had me still bond. My mind had to be renewed and my heart had to be created new and the right spirit had to be dwelled inside of me and my flesh had to die daily, I still had hatred in my heart for my mother for giving me away, I had blamed her for everything that ever happened to me, and I still have no forgiveness toward my uncles and foster parents and any man that ever hurt me, I had a murderous heart because I wanted to kill the man that killed my brother, I had a fornication heart because of the man I had slept with still, I had a rebellious heart because I still wanted to get even with people that ever hurt me, I had a jealous and envy heart because I hated and wanted what other families had with their children and I had a deceitful heart because I still had the secret of my baby girl, I never knew that all these things was hindering me from God true blessings on my life, so now I am taking baby steps all over again learning how to become me. A person God created.

I had a shameful heart because I was ashamed of anyone knowing what happened in my past, I had an unclean heart because of all the evil things I had hid inside, I had to learn how to love and forgive myself first then I could feel my heart being made new, when this started happening then I saw a new child of Christ being made over, and what a beautiful person I started to become, it seemed like I was a total different person in the same body, every where I went and everything I touched was bless, I started to call my mother every mother's day and her birthday and holidays letting her know how me and her grandkids were doing, our relationship was not totally whole yet. But I was working on a relationship with her and God was giving me the strength to over look some of her ways, I was not scared to be in a room with older men, I wanted to help and share my story with foster kids and lost teens that have been abused or anyone that God sent my way, I was proud to share my testimony with others. I had to let them know that God will wipe their tears away. And let them know that with Jesus all things are possible and God can change their night into day, I wanted every one that ever been through some or half or either all of things I been through that the lord will and has heard their cry and they do not haven't to be ashamed of anything that was out of their control but God will and can turn it around for his glory, I wanted to tell the world how God turned my sorrow into joy and to never give up on what God can do. Every time I tell my story I thought about that light I had seen while I was in the coma and to tell you the truth I know now that it was God who had sent an angel dressed as my brother, when God need to get your attention he would use any thing or any one to let you know that you are his, thank you Jesus I could not believe that I could open my mouth up every day to say thank you lord, something that was blocked in me was know opened, when I truly looked back on my life thinking about what I had to do just to feed my children I almost ended up in prison by hanging with people that really did not care about my destiny, I had allow myself to do things that I hated doing, committing fraud with my mother allowing her to mess my life up like she had help my sister do, but through the grace of God I have been given another chance to do this right, now the time has come 1996 my adopter mother had turn for the worst her cancer had got so bad and I had traveled back to Utah at this time to reunite back with my baby girl, a friend called me and told me that they were back there, so I went to visit , and to tell you the truth I loved Utah I never wanted to leave, but it was the sickness that moved me, or maybe it was God! But I could not stay long I had return back to Ohio to care for my adopted mother I was so sad to see her suffer the way she did, I prayed so many days and night that God would ease her pain, I would sit with her and talk with her, she would always let me know that she was so proud of me. I never had any one tell me that they were proud of me, these few words meant a lot to me because she had never told me, and I did not know if I truly mattered but her words were so heart felt, and the next day I was sitting there giving here morphine mediation because she was in so much pain I prayed that God please help her. By taking her home or cure her.

And at that moment she past, I was so hurt but was glad that she did not haven't to suffer no more. At the last hour I had with my adopted mother I had read the bible to her and prayed with her to let her know to give her life to God at that last hour that she had even though I did not know that she was going in that hour, but I know that she ask God to forgive her for all her sins and that she know that Jesus died for her sins, and she invited him in her heart, and that had gave me peace, I never felt that my adopted sisters and brothers were nothing but my real family, that is how close we were, but when my adopted mom past we kind of drifted apart, at this time I was living pay check to pay check even though I had the lord on my side and I was in church I kind of meet another man he was in the church so I really thought it was okay to date and I just knew he was different than the men I have dated in my past, that was the worldly men and this was a spiritual man, lord wasn't I blind to the fact that a man is a man, if he don't allow God to be in control of his flesh, well it was this one night I decided to go over his house to watch a movie with him he had invited me over I did not feel that it would be wrong to do, but I was feeling a feeling not to go, but I thought he is a man of God, what could happen? If only I knew, if only I listen to the voice that was saying no inside. Lord what is going on? I said to myself, this Godly man forced his self on me telling me that I am going to marry you so don't worry, I tried to push him off me but he was to strong it felt like it was deja'vu, lord where did I go wrong? This man a man of God had raped me. What and who can I talk to? Who would believe me? And he felt like there was nothing wrong, like it was okay because he was a man of God or what! I did not go to church for two weeks, and the people of the church kept calling me and because I would not answer they started coming by but I just told them I just was sick with the flu, after a while I did confine in a sister at the church and she told the pastor, so the pastor wanted to have a meeting with me and the brother in the church, so we did and the results was that the pastor had quote a scripture in the bible saying that we cannot take our brethren to the law of the land we haven't to reason together in the church, I was so confuse and could not believe that you can rape someone in the church and just have a meeting in this meeting he also quote another scripture 1 Corinthians chapter 7 that it was better to marry than to burn, it was so hard for me to hold back the tears that were in my heart, I could not believe that they wanted me to marry a man that I did not love and did not know, but I did like him even through what he did was not right all he had to do is confess that he did it and ask for forgiveness and that was all, I really did not know a lot about the word at this time so what ever they told me I believed, I just did not want the lord to turn his back on me again, so what ever I had to do to keep the lord on my side I obeyed the man that had rule over my life he convince us that we should get married because the brother was about to be a minister and they needed him to have a wife before he could be. And the program went on I did what I thought I had to do to make it into the kingdom of God, I did what I thought I had to do for God to be proud of me and to love me, all I wanted was to be save and make it to heaven.

So I married this man, a man the church had choose for me not the one God had for me, the funny thing was we got married on a bible study night, but the pastor did not want us to let anyone know that we were married, I never understood that at all, it was two to three weeks that we had a ceremony, and this is when we were allowed for people and the saints to know, even though I felt like I made the biggest mistake of my life, all I felt was I was not lonely anymore and all I got from him was lust and rejection, I was just happy to know that God was please that I was with my husband and not a man that was not, here it is 2001 and my baby girl had found me through my best friend that lived in Utah she had gave her my phone number, soon as the phone rang I felt some type of feeling I can't explain I heard the voice on the other end I started speaking in tongue glory to God it was my baby girl on the other end, I cried she cried through the whole conversation, and at that moment within a week I had sent for my baby girl and she was here in Youngstown Oh with us, her sister and brother was so happy to see her and I took my baby to church and she gave her life to God, my baby boy had joined the army at this time and was not living here, but she would talk to him on the phone. The lord heard my prayer and sent her back to us, it seemed like we were never apart. Thank you Jesus! So as time went by I enjoyed working in the church I song in the choir, worked being a usher, help clean the church, did tape ministry, and minister to people by being a soul winner for the lord, I read my word daily, I fast and prayed and talk to God all the time, but to tell you the truth I was still hurting inside, I really did not feel loved by this man, I only felt like it was a duty, he would give me a allowance weekly only what the pastor would tell him to give me, fifty dollars, I felt like I was a slave cook clean and have sex that's all it was sex not love only a duty to do as his wife it felt like he would use the bathroom on me because I felt numb all the time I hated it. I asked God to help me love this man, because he was my husband by law. But as time pass by I was getting weary, all he would do is work come home eat and read the bible, where was I at in this make believe marriage? So I started getting restless and started making mistakes and he would tell the pastor every thing even our sex life, well I started reading the word for myself and asking God for wisdom and knowledge and his understanding in his word for me, I just got tired of them telling me what the word mean and what God was saying concerning my life, I started asking questions, and I was told that I was acting rebellious, because I did not agree with some things that they would say, at this time I was helping a lot of children and children with handicaps, so I had took in a young lady that was mentally challenge, and she was going to church with me at this time the pastor wanted to see her in the office and she did not feel comfortable with him alone so she had ask me to sit in some of there sessions, so I let him know that if he wanted to talk to her then I need to be present with her, since I was her guardian, And he told me no, so I would not let him talk with her alone so I got put out the church and was told that they were taking me to court for false statement that I claimed against the pastor, because I refuse to let him talk with her alone, what kind of church that would kick you out for a mistake? And if I did and wanted to ask for forgiveness then I was dome. I really was hurt every one in the church had turned their backs on me, the church members were not allowed to talk with me or pray for me, and to top it all they had the man I was sleeping with turn his back on me, he would separate himself from me, which was fine with me because I really hated sleeping with him and being his slave just by marriage, it had got so bad because I had been through a lot at this time, while I was married to this man, my body had got afflicted, I had became very ill my lungs had collapsed and I had to be on twenty four hour oxygen, due to stress, and not knowing if someone was doing something to me or not, because my test I would get had some type of drug that I was not taking at all. And I had develop stenosis and spondylolisthesis of the spinal and it would paralysis me from the waist down, I ended up in a wheel chair for six months and had to use oxygen for one year, and believe me, I could not understand what in the world I did but it had to be something that the Lord would be mad at me, this is what I was taught in the church that if something bad happen to you while you were walking with God, then you had to do something wrong to deserve it, I never knew that when a person fall short, that the church would turn their back on you and kick you out of the place you need to get help from and to tell people not to pray for you, I thought that I was in a make believe movie. But I knew that It was real after three years of long suffering I was healed from being in a wheel chair and I was healed from being on the oxygen and the marriage was falling apart, I was not his dream robot wife he wanted, shut up and put out, and obey. I really did not care about making this marriage work because I was in a mental abusive, and controlling relationship, I was not allow to think for my self or read the word and understand the wisdom and knowledge God was giving me. I felt like my past was repeating itself and I was getting discourage with no one to talk to, but the people that was of the world. So I found myself slipping back into my old self, at this time my faith in God had decrease instead of increase. So I found myself falling and not knowing how to get back up, you see even though I was saved by grace I felt Like I was out of place, I did not feel the love from God anymore, I knew that God had wiped my tears away from the past, but what about the future ones? I went backwards instead of forward, I was to scared to ask God for forgiveness because of how I was treated by his people I felt that God was the same way. And plus I had messed up so bad that my shame had came back to hunt me, in 2002 I received my divorce, boy I felt just like a failure I had a marriage in the world and it did not work now I am married in the church and it still did not work. I just was so upset with my life I ran from God instead of asking him for his help. I wanted to go back to God but I was to scare of God's rejection. I listen to friends family and even my enemies to mess up my life more, even when I tried to do good it seemed like evil was always present, I tried to live my life like I use to but I felt a strange feeling come over me I could not get any rest, my heart was very troubled so one night I went to a club but after twenty minutes of being there a voice kept telling me I do not belong here so I end up leaving and going home.

I started crying asking God what do you want from me? When I arrived home I sat at my bedside and looked at the bible I had on my bed, I felt if I kept the bible in my bed no man would enter, as I picked up the bible I drop it and the bible had open up to Psalms 34 verse 18 and 19 Saying the lord is nigh unto them that are of a broken heart and saves such as have a contrite spirit, many are the affliction of the righteous, but the lord delivered him out of them all. And then the lord spoke to me in Psalms 147 verse 3 saying he heal the broken in heart and bind up their wounds, so I had relied on these words every day, and found my self asking God again to forgive me, I repented of my sins once again I thought that God would be tired of me by now, Using him as a revolving door, in and out, this time I was faithful I stared going to church again I was Scared at first thinking about the church I was in before, the enemy had made me feel like a failure because being divorce twice was not acceptable in the church, and then came my shame again feeling I had set a bad example for my children and the people I were ministry too, I was feeling my self abandoned and rejected so here I go again maybe I thought to myself that I was only suppose to go to a certain point of my life and then that was it. Was I ever going to find true happiness and have God love me they way he love others I wondered. As I started reading my word morning noon and night I started asking God to help me understand, and to give me his knowledge and wisdom, I ask God to create in me a new heart and restore the right spirit in me, I needed to be delivered from everything in my past I found myself repenting every day even if I did not felt I sin I repented I just wanted my mind to be renewed. I found out by God that it takes more than going the church on Sunday and working in the church to be delivered, it took me developing a personal relationship with God myself to find out who I am in him, it was a process for me to see his hand in my life, not the overnight makeover I had in the church, I realize that I was not going to be perfect but I can work on perfection, I needed to face that little girl in my past and let her know that we can move on with Christ all things are possible, the word of God had taught me that I needed to study to show myself approve to God not man, all the time that I thought that I was dome from the start, how I allowed the enemy to conversant in my hear daily, I could not hear from God when I had myself in bondage, I was caught up in what people thought of me and how people would except me, I forgot that I was still alive, I never was healed because I never forgave my mother it was still hurt in my heart concerning her when ever I go through some type of trail I would blame her and my father and the foster parents and my uncles and everyone that ever done me wrong, there was a corner in my heart that still would not forgive, as I study my bible the lord spoke to me in his word in Ephesians chapter 4 verse 32 his speaks about being kind to one another, even as God for Christ sake forgiven you, I never allowed my self to move from milk to the meat of the word, I allow man to give me what the word said and never took the time to read it for myself, what ever man said concerning my life I believed that is what God said about and for me, not that God has not talk to them but I never took the time to ask God myself. I have always looked at the word through mans and the love I needed, I thought if a man or Godly man loved me than I was okay but all it did was send me backwards to the problems I had from the very beginning.

Looking for love to wipe my tears away in all the wrong places I was headed in the right direction but I turned in the wrong arms. I thought being married would of solve some of the tears, but I was seeking love from the wrong source, the word of God in Matthew 6 verse 33 told me to seek the kingdom of God first and his righteousness and these things shall be added. I allowed the enemy to set up so many traps for me to fall in because of my lack of knowledge in his word. At this time it was a new year 2004 I had learn to live on my own and get a relationship with God. I felt pretty strong in God, I felt I was in the right place with God and I felt that God loved me and I was in a good church with a good pastor, that had a heart after God's own heart, I was working in the church again loving what I was doing and loving God for giving me another chance, my new year I just began and I was sure that the tears were being wiped away until a called came in from Utah at this time my baby girl had went back to Utah and the call had caught me off guard I was in the middle of praising the lord and a sister took me in the back to let me know that I had a emergency call, this call changed my life I never thought that something like this would ever happen to me my world stopped at that moment I was on pause and then it seemed like my life did a rewind, my daughter had been murdered! My baby girl had lost her life, was I dreaming? Was someone playing a trick on me? Was this April's fool? Lord tell me what is going on, I screamed out to God over and over again, everyone tried to pray and hold me up, but I did not want any thing I did not want them to say one word about God what kind of God would keep my life like a roller coaster? I was so angry, I hated the whole world, I just could not understand why me? That was all I wanted to know from the lord, nothing else, I wanted God to show his face to me. I thought that I was going to loose my mind, why are you keeping me sane lord? Why are you keeping me healthy lord? Why are you keeping me on this place you call earth lord? Why do you want me lord? I had so many questions for God, but it seemed like he could not hear me. Or did he just plug his ears to my cry this time? I allowed myself to go in a place that was darker than I ever could imagine, I shut down all together if God would not kill me, than I would never eat! Then maybe I would stave to death! Pills would not kill me, cancer could not kill me, a coma could not kill me, my not walking could not kill me, my lungs could not kill me, me being raped, molested, rejected, abandoned, shamed, could not destroy me, than maybe if I just fade away God would let me go. I just did not care any more; I turned my back on the word of God and everything that had to do with God. I was so angry and mad that I shut my heart down to feel, I could not bury my baby girl and keep loving a God that I felt did not love or care for me, was his word just a big lie? I just did not care. I went back to the life I was use too, a life of pain. After loosing a child I felt like God was punishing me for not letting my children know the truth I wanted too lord knows I did, but my best friend had went through all legal process to have my baby girl legally and she never kept her from us, and the kids knew that they were brothers and sisters from their spirit I really did not want to upset the family ties that we all had. Maybe hiding this secret cost me no matter how much I asked for forgiveness, did I really come clean and let it all out for God to fix?

I had also read in his word that God can not be mark, there is nothing under the sun that God don't know he is a all knowing and all seeing God, after hating myself and mad at the world and harming myself, my son in Germany sent for me to come there for a while to get away from things and to clear my head. So I went to Germany for about two or three months to get away from people, places and things, but did I really? Even though it was so nice to get away, my problems followed me I woke up feeling the same way I felt at home, and I was in a different country trying to run from God, and here he was, here. I had wondered to my self where did I go wrong, I am serving God with all my heart mind and soul, I was giving him all that I had in me trying to live right, praying, fasting, going to church, doing everything I was told to do, where did I go wrong? Here I am a failure in my walk with God, I can't even serve God! Right, I said to myself, I have failed my kids, God and my marriage again. I never wanted to live because if I tried to live life was going to let me down, no matter what. I was just a laughing vessel for entertainment. Was there really love for me? Was there ever going to be someone like my brother who loved me through it all? At this point I really did not care before I left the states I had slipped back into a backsliding position, I was going out again and living like I never knew God, but something in me made me feel convicted, I felt strange, like I was in a place I never knew. I felt like I was heading for danger but I really did not care, I was out one night with a couple of friends and I met this guy, he had asked me what was I doing in a place like this because I don't seem like the type that hangs out in clubs? And at this point of my life I really did not care I answered him by saying looks are deceiving, we talked for a while and just before he walked away he said to me don't allow your identity be what the world haven't to offer, and know that there is one person that really cares about them tears! I was stunned because how did he know about my tears? Who was this guy? I never meet him before, when I turned around to see where he went I could not find him, I walked around the club at least a dozen times and he was no where to be found. I felt a strange feeling, and wanted to leave I told my friends that I was not feeling well and I wanting to go home. I thought about them words all the way home and on my way to Germany, wondering who was this man? Who sent him? It was so strange, I just could not shake them words no matter how hard I tried. I had more questions for this guy and never got his name or number. So I t was time to leave Germany I had a good time and enjoyed being with my grandkids and daughter-in-law and my son, it was great, but my tears were still heavy and still there. My mind was still in a state of confusing, I had grew to love this God and I feared his word and did not understand why I had to go through so much in my life. Know it is 2005 a new year again I was back home I just arrived I unpacked my suitcases and the doorbell rang and it was a sister from the old church I first gave my life to God, the church that hurt me deeply, I wondered what did she want I loved her a lot we were like sisters, she was my foster sister at a time and I loved her two daughters she asked me how was I doing and I let her know that I just got back from Germany visiting my baby boy and his family, and she gave me a hug and said that she loved me and was praying for me, I looked shocked because the church we were at together did not want them to talk with me or pray for me, they felt that I was a lost cost, a bad seed, so I could not understand what she wanted from me.

I asked her don't you believe that my bad spirit would rub off on you, and she laugh and said I want you go come to church with me, I told her you must be crazy they do not want me at that church I am not allowed on the church grounds, She said I don't go there any more I go to a new church, I said no, because when I really needed Her she had turned her back on me, because of what man told her to do, and if I mess up again she would do it again, and I did not want to go through the rejection any more, but we talk she apologized for how she treated me and ask for forgiveness and told me she loved me and God had sent her to invite me to this church, oh boy what do God want from me again? I said to myself, so after a few begs I said what do I haven't to loose, so I said yes, I still was feeling the pain of loosing a child and from a failed marriage, and not having a relationship with my mother, losing two brothers and not forgiving my father before he had past and I just had lost an uncle I loved dearly, and the lost of the only mother I had my adopted mother, and a nephew, my pain was so deep inside I was to scared to let anyone in I was scared to be put out another church I felt that I was marked with some type of seal, letting people know that I was a lose cost from birth. I knew if I did not get myself together I was going to head down a road of destruction and instead of disappointing God again I rather die, and go to hell, so I started plotting my death again, I knew that I was weak and was scared to ask man to pray for me, I did not have enough strength to pray for myself, every time I tried I felt worst, so I deciding writing letters to my kids letting them know everything concerning my life and letting them know how much I loved them, and about their baby sister. I knew that she was coming to get me for church and I wanted to be gone before she arrived so I got some pills together, and got myself together, I read my bible before I decided to end all this pain, I wrote the letters to my kids, and then

I had a long talk with God, I really did not know if God was listening or not, but I cried out anyway for the last time, right before I took over 95 pills, saying lord please forgive me for all I was not to you, forgive me for all my sins, I know I would never be with you, or feel your hug or kiss, God I really did not want much, I did not want fame or riches, I did not want silver or gold, I did not want a house or a mansion, lord all I wanted was your love and forgiveness, lord all I wanted is you to be proud of calling me your child, lord all I wanted was your love if I had your love God nothing in this world would of ever mattered, I am sorry lord that all I have been was a problem child, lord I understand why you never blessed me or kept me, I am so sorry for the mess, I tried to clean it up lord, but it was to messy for me to handle alone, I am so sorry for reopening your wound, I know that you died for me so that I could have life, and all I ever done was brought you shame! But God I did believe you at your word and feared you that is why I rather died and go to hell then to bring rottenness to your bones, lord my favorite scripture in your word is Proverbs 12 and verse 4 I wanted to be that virtuous woman, because if I was I would have been a crown to you, thank you for giving me another chance and I love you, I really do, lord if I never see you please believe from the depths of my soul and the purity of my heart I am sorry for my wrong doing, and please give your son Jesus a kiss from me if that is not to much to ask for, in Jesus name, after I prayed that prayer to the lord I took all my pills, I had taken 25 blood pressure pills, 30 pain pills, and 30 sleeping pills, I cut off all my lights and unplugged my phone and got into bed and my last words were. God I rather die and go to hell then to live and sin against you again forgive me for I know not what I have done in Jesus name! and I went to sleep.

Then I heard a voice say arise! Real firm it had shook my whole body! Then the voice came again saying arise my child, your faith have made you whole, pick up your cross and follow me and never look back, for my love for you is greater than you can ever bare, all you sins have been forgiven and thrown in the sea of forgetfulness, for I have great works for you, and I know all about you and the tears you have shed before time, even before you were conceived in your mother belly, I gave you life to have it to the fullness, your weeping has endue for a night now your joy will be this morning, praise me in all that you do, tell everyone that Christ has risen in you, tell everyone of my goodness, for my child your life is only in my hands, for the things you have endue was not to harm you but to make you strong and build you up for the purpose I have planned for you. Fret not of evildoers, but in all your ways acknowledge me and I will direct your path. Lean not unto your own understanding but allow me to lead you and guide you the rest of the way, I loved you that's why I have chastening you for a long time! Live again with the peace I am giving you, and live again in my name, I thought I was dreaming, until a bright light shine directly at me like I never seen before, I got up and started pitching myself to make sure I was not dead or dreaming, I started making phone calls to my love ones to see if this was real, I knew I had not gone to the hospital to have my stomach pumped, or I did not vomit the medicine or anything up, I looked around and my floors were clean, I looked at all three bottles and they were empty, I knew that I had taken the pills and being a nurse myself I knew that there was no way I could survive this with out going to the hospital or something! So I got my blood pressure cuff out, and took my pressure it was one forty over eighty my temperature was normal and my skin was bright and shinny, I was walking and talking in my right mind, I started to shout out loud, giving God the glory saying lord you really love me, you really love me, I danced all through the house I wanted to tell everyone one what God had done for me, I knew if I told a doctor they would think that I was lying, or crazy, so I just got ready still looking for any signs of medical problem, a loud knock came at the door, it was my foster sister coming for me to go to the new church, she said you look different , I smiled and got my coat and could not wait to get in a church a shout and testify about Gods miracle, and what the lord has done in me over and over again, as we drove to the church she said to me the lord told me that you are his anointed and he was going to use you in a mighty way, I laugh and said I receive that and believe that like I never done before. As we enter into the new church I felt like I have been here before every one was so nice and I felt good entering into the church everyone gave me a hug like they knew that God had done something in my life. Testimonies had started and I could not wait until I could scream out his blessing over me, I started to say something but the spirit of God was all over me, and I just could not contain myself, I praised the lord all over the church, I think I shouted out over a hundred times thank you lord, and giving him all the glory. And even danced my clothes off.

This was serious and personal for me; I praised the lord all that week. I loved reading Psalms, I loved how David was so grateful of Gods Blessing over his life and for giving him another chance I felt just like that. I knew that God was not silent toward me any more, and the lord never walked away from me, I walked away from him. The lord loved me enough to save me from myself. I had been walking in darkness to long now my eyes were opened and I could see much brighter, in Matthew the lord lets us know that the gate is straight and narrow and if we go our way we would head for destruction, and that was what I was doing because I allowed my past to choose who and what I was and going to be, know I have a song in my heart, a dance in my feet and a shout in my mouth, because God told me in Hebrews chapter 12 verse 6 for whom I love I chasten, I knew then I was truly loved by God. I found out that I had Agape love, unconditional, unselfish, love no matter what I have done in my life, he never turned his back on me, God is a forgiving God and Jesus had already died for the sins I did or going to do, he told me that in Romans chapter 3 verse chapter 23 that all have sinned and come short of the glory of God, and I thought that I was the only bad seed in the bunch, this is how I was miss leaded by man. I was rejected and abandoned and judge every time I made a mistake, rather it was big or small. The lord was talking to me everyday I could hear his voice clearly, and he was letting me know in Psalms chapter 118 verse eight it is better not to put all your trust and confidence in man but put in the lord. The lord had let me know that he was the only one that knows the plans he has for me, and he wants to prosper me, and not harm me, but to give me hope and a future in him. As I read my word daily he spoke this to me in Jeremiah chapter 29 verses 11. It was so hard in my past to hear from God when I first gave my life to him because I was moving faster than my spirit was taking me. The lord let me know that I got to be still and see the salvation of the lord work in my life and it was a process not when I want it, but when I needed it, it was going to be on time. I need to grow in God and be in my proper place at the proper time, to see the works of God manifest in my life. I need a real solid foundation relationship with the lord so when the trails and tribulations come I would be in a firm position that when I fall I would be able to get right back up. I joined the church and was growing daily with my the studies they had, and the studies I were doing at home with God, I was falling in love with the lord and learning how to love and forgive, starting with myself I had to forgive myself first, then I found myself forgiving my mother, father, foster parents, uncles, and even the men that hurt me in my life and took advantage of me. The lord was teaching me how to love myself, and to be a person he had made me to be in his own image. I had to start back with that little girl, the lord showed me in his word. In Genesis chapter one verse twenty six, he states lets make man in his own image, in his likeness for God to make me in his own image, I know that I was very special. God told me that I had to be tested and go through some things because of the call I had over my life.

And then I read the story concerning Job in the bible the word then spoke to me letting me know that if Satan could destroy me, the purpose that was already planned for my life would not be, only if I gave up and not believe, if Job went through everything I read in the word of God how he believed and had faith to know that no matter what comes or go he would trust in the lord till the day he die, and then how his trust in God bless him more than he was, then why can't I hang in there a little while longer knowing that the enemy works are to seek as a thief comes to steal, and kill, and to destroy, and this is what he had set out for me as a child to steal my identity by letting my mind believe that I was dome from the start allowing me to believe I was ugly, nothing to myself or anyone else, and everyone would look at me as a trouble problem child, I was believing that I would never be a child of God, I tried to kill myself by taking my own life, I felt neglected, abandoned, I was emotionally, mentally and physically abused, I was trick to believe I was full of lust, loneliness, envy, jealousy, full of lies, but thank the lord he had his hand on my life all along. As I spent more time with God I received my learning and the word taught me daily by killing my flesh daily, I know that the devil would try to discredit the lord's word and his job was to destroy that belief, in John chapter five verse thirty six tells us that if we believe of his son we will have everlasting life, and Acts chapter sixteen verse thirty one also let us know to believe in the lord Jesus Christ we shall be save and our household, this last attempt I have been running for the lord it is know 2006 and every thing is good

I still been having trials and tribulations but reading my word daily fasting and praying and talking to God developing the relation I need with him falling in love with my lord and savoir it has been three years and living alone with out a man in my life was great, I meet a good man of God my bible study partner we loved doing ministry for the lord and a man that was really after God's own heart, this walk with God was sweeter than the day before, one day I was going to the store and was at the counter and a man behind me ask for change and I turned around to give him a dollar and it was the man that had took my brother life, the brother that I loved dearly, my heart beat but all I could do is hand him the dollar and walked to my car with feeling compassion for him, I sat in my car for a minute and thanked God because at a time in my life I had planned to kill this man for taking someone I love so dearly away, the enemy tried me at this moment wanting me to run him over with my car, but I called on the name of Jesus to give me strength as he walked out the store I asked him if he needed a ride and he got in my car not knowing or remembering that I was the sister of the man he killed, I asked him was he saved and he said no, I told him that God loves him and forgave him and I forgive him too, he looked at me and remembered and said you are tee-bone sister and I said yes with a tear in his eye he said I am so sorry, pray for me. And I gave him a hug and gave him a church to go to and told him don't let it be too late. I knew then that God was making a change in my life, after hating this man for so many years, I could not find that hate I had all I felt was compassion for him and wanted to help this man, Glory be to God.

I thank God all the way home, because if God did not step in right on time, I would have been in prison or somewhere, thank you lord for saving me. I prayed all that week for that young man that God bless him, I knew then I was changed. My mind was being renewed and God was still working on me. As a child I did not realize that God had his hand on my life, all I ever seen was the darkness that was given to me no light that shine in my life. I am an older woman now with grown children and grandchildren and just experiencing true love a love that no other could give or show a love that God gave his only begotten son so I can have this life. I am having now, what a love that someone could show to lay down his life for his people, not my mother, nor my father, not my brother or sister, friends nor any of my family ever shown or gave this type of love. To know that God has set us up in heavenly places with Jesus Christ some day, you see all the time he loved me, but when you are in darkness and have not seen any light you cant see, feel or taste any love, only temporary loves that comes and goes all the time. But the love from God is real he will never turn his back on you he loved me through it all, when I was not patience, when I did not want to repent, when I was being bad, when I shut the door on him, when I served Satan time after time after time, even when I didn't even love myself, he loved me, even when I cursed my life he had given me, he loved me even when I thought that I have accomplished things on my own, he loved me, even when I told him that I hated him, he loved me, when I spited on him, laughed at him, and even nailed him to the cross by rejecting who he was, denying his love for me, the lord never gave up on me. I can tell you this because he forgave me, he protected me, he trust me with his word, because he believed in me, because he preserved my soul, because he never failed me yet, because he threw all my sins in the sea of forgetfulness. I was a broken vessel and the lord looked down from heaven and breath life of everlasting in me, the devil had to get permission to do what he had done, but the lord demanded him like he did Job don't take her life, just to know that made me realize that God never left my side, now tell me who do you know that will stand by you all the way? Grace and mercy has followed me all the days of my life, and still is today. if we don't have hope then what do we have? I always heard growing up keep hope alive? That's true but with out keeping Jesus alive in you then you got no hope to keep. All I had to do is repent ask God to forgive me and live the way he design for me to live, study my word, develop a relationship with the lord, receive Christ in my life, believe his word, then I would be born again, then I would receive the instruction on how to overcome the affliction that would attack my flesh because the spirit would fight my battle for me, all I had to do is surrender the dark pain I had reserved for the devil and give it to Jesus, I could of saved myself a lot of unnecessary chaos. Even we believe in God then why is so hard to believe him at his word? Our knowledge is not the knowledge of God, but we can receive it, in Matthew Chapter seven verse eight says everyone that asked received so ask for knowledge ask for wisdom ask for understanding God will open the door for you and Gods people is being destroyed ever day because of being fools to the lack of knowledge.

If we would just pick up our bibles everyday and read more than a Sunday or Bible study night than we would find more treasures to our solutions on dealing with daily traumas, Yes God gives to the pastors, leaders, prophets, teachers, evangelists, but he also gives to you, so that your spirits would come into agreements on where God is taking and bringing you from, second Timothy chapter two verse fifteen tells us to study to show thyself approved only unto God, so that we would not be blind or deceived by the enemy traps by false Prophets that will come in the name of Jesus Christ. I was so guilty of that, I would go to church listen to what the pastor preached and on and TV ministries and just read daily bread and hearing the word through other people, I was just to lazy to pick up my bible and read for myself, the lord had to show me that you just don't go out and eat from everyone breakfast, lunch, dinner or snack table, we need to prepare are own food so that we can put in the right ingredients so we will be able to digest it the right way and the taster the spiritual man would be able to know that we can cook too. I had to remember that I was being prepared to be God's bride, and how would I want to come prepared? Done or under cooked? As I allow my spiritual man to be fed the right things I seen a change and growth on how I dealt with my trails and tribulations, Matthew chapter twenty verse fourteen tells us that many are called but only a few are chosen to lead God's people, so it is very important to read and study the word daily so when the test come you would not faint or give in, when I starting letting go and let God I started seeing my tears being wiped away, it was so hard for me to believe that the word of God was real because I have seen so many leaders and family members mock the word so much, until God manifest him self to me, the lord has opened up my eyes everyday and the light gets brighter and brighter everyday. I have put my trust in man to long, believing when they tell me I am not save I believe it, when I made mistakes over and over again I was not a child of God, I believe it, when I spoke my mind when my spirit did not agree what they would say concerning my life, I was rebellious, I believed it, in their eyes I was not good enough or I was another failure because I did not walk, talk, jump or say how high, I did not look a certain way, I was not important enough, I believed it. But the

Lord let me know a different song to the dance in his word Ephesians chapter two verse five says His Grace saves me, and in Romans chapter three verse twenty-three he also tells me that we all have sinned and Come short of the glory of God, I am not what man says I am but I am what God says I am and that is I am more than a conqueror because of his love, what a great identity to receive from God himself, thank you Jesus. All thing are new and the old is past away, I can look at life the way God had me to look at it through his eyes, my tears still come but I can rejoice the lord has turned my sorrow into joy, I had no faith, I had no joy, I had no hope and no peace, but look at me know I got the victory, sometimes we got to be broken so that we realize that we can not be made whole again until receive and believe that we need Jesus, when I look back over my life as a little girl I can truly say I am bless, when I look back over my life as a young woman I can say I am truly bless, when I look back over my life as a woman today I can truly say that I am bless, and I got a testimony to share to this world. If you don't believe that Satan is reality then keep reading this book over and over and over until you get it, but know that God is real.

And the lord is still working on me, he is washing me daily, you see I was just living my life in a way I thought was pleasing to me to be happy, but all I was doing was destroying my destiny with filthy things inside of me and believe me it was many, I had an abuse spirit, adultery spirit, anger spirit, anxiety spirit, low self esteem spirit, attitude spirit, backsliding spirit, bad habit spirit, bitterness spirit, deceit spirit, depression spirit, discouragement spirit, doubt spirit, enemies spirit, envy spirit, fame spirit, fear spirit, flattery spirit, gambling spirit, gossip spirit, grief spirit, guilt spirit, incest spirit, laziness spirit, loneliness, spirit, lust spirit, occult spirit, pride spirit, revenge spirit, self pity spirit, shame spirit, lying spirit, and the list goes on, some times we believe that we go to church and one thing we think that we are that we are okay, but the devil is a lie every time we turn our backs on God and go another way we picks up more demons spirits and it is more harder than when we first gave our live to Christ, some of us now feel that we are okay because no one around us knows are deep dark secrets, and we set down on someone's else deliverance because of that fear we have deep down inside to not let oursefs be totally free from shame, their will be and are not any perfect families, but we can building into Gods family that can be made into perfection if we let go and let God, God can heal all broken vessels. It does not take over night for your process to happen but if you put your time in believe me payday is on the way, stop going to these get your miracles today and that's it, and go to the real place God's house, and wait on your blessing! Romans chapter 14 verse 12 the lord tells that everyone shall give an account of him or her self to him no matter what someone else has done or said to you, and read second Corinthians chapter five verse ten everyone may receive the things done in his or her body according to what our actions, are whether it is good or bad, and every time I backslid I gave the enemy more closet space to hang his garments for me to wear, know that the flesh got to die daily but your soul is what God demands the devil not to touch, so go through it is worth it at the end, it is very hard to suffer but know that the longsuffering is molding you into the image of God and in his likeness. Just know that the fruit is being replanted from bad soil to good soil and this time when it grows it is going to bloom into the flower we were meant to be in the beginning planned time, God's time. I decided that I rather be born twice than to die once. It is so funny I remember when I first came to Jesus I heard this song come to Jesus come to Jesus come to Jesus right now, he will save me from all I went through and going through they let me believe that I would not suffer any more I would not shed a tear any more, he has forgiven me, and all my problems were gone, My life would be so much better, no more worries; all my troubles would be over, I would have peace joy and happiness I would be bless with lots of things, and all I heard was just that, but they forgot to let me know that Jesus had paid for all that and then some with his blood by being beaten, lied on, talked about, spit on, dragged, rejected, tempted, and nailed to his cross that he had to carry, the enemy hated Jesus so what make us think that we did not have a cross to carry!

As long as you are living for the lord you got to bear the same things, but yes you would and can be able to endue it all, but only with the strength of God, we are save by his grace and by him giving his life for us. And we got to give something in return, ourselves, this flesh do not mean us no good, pick up your cross no matter how hard it is, and allow Jesus to help you carry it to the end, we have a test to go through, a test that helps us to our destiny, Don't let the devil defeat you, know that

God is the master of all, and he knows what he needs to do to get us where we need to go, and where we need to be, first Peter chapter one verse seven tells us that our trails of our faith being more precious than anything that perish going through the fire might be praise and honor and glory when Jesus comes for you, and Revelation Chapter two verse ten tell us not to fear none of these things that we suffer it is the devil job to cast some of us into prison that we be tried and have tribulations, but for us to be faithful because God has a great crown of life for us, the enemy wants us to believe that we will not make it, this is it for us, but we no that Satan is the father and creator of lies and the truth was and not in him. Hold on to the little faith that you got and allow God to uncover your victory, I am still holding on waiting and enjoying my walk with the lord, yes I am still going through, yes I have fallen short, yes my mind wonders if I am going to make it, but when I truly think about the goodness of Jesus and all that he has brought me from and see the true call on my life my soul just screams toward the finish line, by me studying the word of God and developing a relationship with the lord helped saved my life, reading Psalms chapter five verse 3 trained me how to ask God for his help. Reading Lamentations Chapter three verse twenty-three helps me to know Gods faithfulness and how his mercy I need everyday. Because when my trails comes it would only be the test of my faith in him, oh believe me it will still come until that day, Of the lord return, but know that the battle is already won. There is a road that we need to follow called the highway to heaven, and it is straight and narrow there are no left or right turns but if you get side tracked you can make a u – turn and get back on the right road, so when the persecution occur know that it is only planed to build the faith of the image we see a head, Jesus! Every day I got to give him the praise no matter what I am going through knowing that I was nothing but a dirty filthy rag, and God is using me as a precious gift wrapped with a lot of blessings that is precious in his sight. All my life I was program to believe that I was a walking dead to late to help human being, the devil had me wrapped up tangle up in sin, but the escape was the key of choice! God had hand delivered it to me in the right box called you shall live and not die, I remember when I came out of the coma people would ask me about life after death, and I really did not know how to answer that, until now, I am life after death a new woman in Christ,

I was dead to sin now I am alive in Christ, having love, joy, peace, longsuffering, gentleness, goodness, faith, meekness, and temperance. You know every time I think about where the lord has brought me from, the things I go through now should be easy but sometime we forget the blessings his mercy and his grace, when other trails come, I know when I was being afflicted with being in a wheelchair, being bed bond, or on twenty four hours oxygen, when my body was so bend up into knots, when my body was racking with pain, I was on every medication that was new on the market that they could give me, when I had several nervous breakdowns being depressed, people betting on my life rather I was going to live or die.

When people wonder why haven't I lost my mind yet. It was all God. Second Peter chapter two verse twenty four tells us that Jesus himself bared our sins in his body on the tree that we being dead to sins, should live unto righteousness, and by his stripes we are healed, I was already healed before my time, whatever afflictions my flesh endued is dead, and cannot do me any harm I am healed through Christ that dwells in me. And when I thought that hope was all gone, when I was not accepted and my church family turned their backs on me I thought I would not be accepted into another church, by having my name slandered and being an social outcast, the lord gave me comfort in the mist of it all, and minister to my soul with Romans chapter ten verse eleven for whosoever believe in me shall not be ashamed, and Psalm chapter fifty five verse twenty two cast all your burdens upon me said the lord and I shall sustain you, the lord would never let me suffer for his righteous to be removed, when we are being cursed we will be bless, when we are being persecuted we can endue it, when we are being slander for his name sake we answer kindly. For the battle is not ours it is the lords. Being a divorce woman bothered me a lot until the lord let me know that I need to be married to him first. And be taught how to become a wife, I needed more cleansing from my past, more training, more molding, I need to know how to love myself first, be faithful, be loyal, be honest, be patient, be wise, be obedient, and longsuffering I had to be approved and sealed by God first and believe me I had none of these things not even a crumb, some of us get married because of past failure like me, loneliness, lust, finance for all the wrong reason but how can you love and want to spend your life with someone when you hate ourselves ? And we lack all our time with God, we can't even be in a relation with God so how can we do it with a man or female? We need to call on the clean up power and that is God. So we will not be left behind when the lord appears. I received peace after my divorce the lord is doing a great work in me so know that I am still in training with the spirit of God to be what I need to be for my maker, my creator, if you want a husband or seeking to be a wife this is what God told me in Isaiah chapter fifty for verse five thy maker is the husband the lord of host is his name, and thy redeemer, the holy one, the God of the whole earth shall he be called, so every time I get a itch form someone saying little nothing in my ear I remember the word First Corinthians chapter six verse eighteen through twenty tells me to flee from fornication, every one that commits fornication sinned against his own body, and that our bodies are the temple in which the holy spirit dwells in and the holy spirit does not dwells in an unclean temple, and that we do not belong to God. We are brought with a price so therefore glorify God in your body and in your spirit just like his word say in first Thessalonians chapter four verse three this is the will of God, that we should abstain from fornication and believe me it might be hard but it is worth it when you know that in James chapter one verse twelve tells us that bless is the man the endured temptation for when he is tried, he shall receive the crown of life which the lord hath promised to them that love and keeps his commandments. And believe me it is still a battle, but I refuse to turn back now or give up, the lord has brought me to far, for me to not hold on just a little longer.

This is why it is so important for us that go through or have been through so much turmoil's in our past or present to tell yourself, train yourself, to feast on the word morning noon and night, even for a midnight snack, so that when the enemy arise with some type of mess you will be able to reset and make a stand from what is right, go through but don't entertain. I had to do the same thing and still calling on the lord name, long but I thank God every time I wake up, and decided to follow Jesus through it all. We have a cover if we want it, and that is the blood of Jesus, and believe me there is a warning precautious Sign telling us to stop, yield, don't go, or enter at your own risk! We cannot put down any part of the whole Armor of God, for any reason! How can you go to battle with good looks, or holding your sword the word your bible, sometimes your hands need to be free that is why we need the word in our hearts so that when the enemy comes at you and see you empty handed you are equipped in heart, mind and soul, and know that you need it everyday when you walk with God! When you start your journey toward your destiny don't start tired, sleepy and unprepared, like the five fool less virgins, have your lamp full, let your light shine all the way, until you get to your destination. Because the enemy hates to lose and he will keep coming back, he wants to destroy your destiny your purpose your plan that God has for you, and be on guard but fret not there is nothing he can do to you that God has not okayed, he needs permission, so look! If he got permission to attack, then know that God has elevated you to overcome. Don't think that I have it all together because I don't, but I got someone in my corner that does! Jesus Christ! What more do I need? It is now late 2006 and I had a flood come toward me my faith was being tried again my real biological mother was ill I was running up and down the high way from Ohio to New York seeing about her I really did not know what was wrong I had started a ministry for the youth in my community back in 2005 sharing some of my testimony spending time teaching them about God and having children Church, it was so fulfilling with no help from others just doing what the lord put in me to do to share the love of Jesus to these children was awesome. I used all my disability check monthly for uniforms supplies, gas, food, and field trips to these youth I did not care what it cost me I did what my heart lead me to do, some were children from bad and good back ground we help elderly, we went to hospitals, nursing home and group homes to share the love of Jesus, I would load up 20 kids in a little car I had and just prayed that the Lord provide us there and back, it was sad that my community never step in to give a hand, but I was not discouraged I pushed my self with God on my side and did what I had to do, with going back and fourth to New York it was hard people did not care to step in to help a small group of children that needed love and compassion, I guess it was to much work, but I did what I had to do, my mother got sicker and I decided to bring her here instead to care for her at my home, the doctors did not believe she would make it that far but I put all my trust in the lord and knew that God still had something for me and my mother to do. And that was build a relationship, before my next ministry that was coming around the corner building families in forgiving their past and parents, God had called me to teach women from all types of family problems. I knew this was a set up from God to build my mother relationship and me because how can I teach something I have not been through myself!

Because we never spent time together and forgave one another, I always loved my mother deep down inside, no matter what she did or said or did not do for me. It was something I needed to move forward to the calling God had for me. Believe me my family was not to thrill about me bringing my mother here, because of some past hidden pain they never faced, but God help me do the right thing, because I had some deep pain inside that was hunting me, and hindering me from moving forward, even though thing were going great in ministry I still had some tears that were still trying to be wiped. I still blamed her for the death of my brother, my rape and being molested, for my failed relationship with men, my failure of being a good mother, my failure of never having a relationship with family members, for me not loving myself and me hating her, I still had some hidden scares, even through God has given me another chance and delivered me from, I still had this deep dark tear that would not leave I needed a mother, touch, love and approval. Why because in Gods word he lets us know that he is the father to the fatherless and a mother to the motherless. So I went and got my mother and had to deal with a lot of medical problems, but I did what I had to do as her child and a child of God I wanted all my actions to be pleasing to God so I prayed daily for the strength of God to help me do the right thing, with out any bitterness in my heart, my baby sister was here at the time, but she was on drugs and she could not be of good help, my mother had sisters but because of past pain it stop them from stepping in like they needed to, so I prayed and did what my heart told me to do, and that is forgive first, love and be the child of God I am, I hated to see her in so much pain in and out of the hospital I really had my hands full with the ministry my relation with God and my children and grandchildren, and taking care of my health to, and a sick mother, God just stepped in and gave the extra hand I needed. I cried many of days because my mother heart was still harden toward me, I screamed because what ever and how ever I did it she would complain, I got angry because she would lie and backbit against me, but I did not sin against her, she made feel like she still hated me, but God held my hand he lifted me up and carried me through it all, she would cause division between me and my children and my baby sister, but God kissed me and sang a new song to me, she spit all type of venom at me, but God washed me and gave me the strength and courage to hold on. In spite of what was fighting her and that was the enemy was doing, the lord had me minister to her daily and show her that her anger and pain that she had was only her test to pull through or be destroy in it, and God wants to deliver her so that he can bless her and heal you from all your infirmities, it was so hard for me to bath, feed and nursery a woman that seemed to hate me, my grandmother never agreed for me to care for my mother, but she still prayed for me. Some of my aunts wanted me to put her in a nursing home and I remember my baby sister said to me sis it is better you than me to care for her, but God had order this day, this time. And this season, for his reasons and I followed his instructions. as time went by I was still doing the ministry the lord had birth in me then he took the ministry to another level. But when you are going through things and others are taking you through, some times the enemy would allow you to think that your past is back and having you doubt God at his word.

Sometimes he would make you believe that this is the worst test you are going through, but know that It is only a test of your faith the higher you go, the higher the devil need to pull you down, because he is no longer welcome in heaven, and when you are going through everyone that give you advice to fail is gone but know that God would never leave you nor forsake you. He will be there through the good and the bad, one morning I was going through and wanted to totally give up with caring for my mother and the lord spoke to me through his word. Deuteronomy chapter thirty one verse six, he said be of good courage, fear not, nor be afraid of them, for the lord thy God do good in me he will never fail me nor fake me, and in Romans chapter fifteen verse thirteen he said that he will fill me with Joy and Peace in my Deliverance I would have hope through the power of the Holy Ghost that is in me. And then he went on by saying in Philippians chapter four verse seven that his peace would give me understanding and God will guard my heart and my mind as long as I keep my belief on him. The lord was so busy helping me that day building my faith up in him, I knew that my mother would be okay and I would too, and to love her through it all, my grandmother always said just love the hell out of people, and if I had to love the hell out of my mother and love Jesus in her then that was my plan to hang in there. Because in Isaiah chapter twenty-six verses three the lord will give me perfect peace just trust him, when I started looking over the hills, which comes my help that my help was only going to come from the lord. Now it is time to slow down a little in ministry I was kind of mad because I loved getting up and doing for Others, but the condition of my mother was getting in greater need, and God was doing a thing with us both He was moving me into another level in ministering to woman and I was getting woman that was not in good relation ships with their Mothers and I was not there yet with my own, so how could the blind lead the blind so I removed myself to get what Jesus needed for me to have before I moved into my next assignment, at this time I had meet a young man that was interested in me, I meet him at a church singing and the lord spoke to me at this time letting me know that this man was my husband and I laugh at the lord saying lord I have no time for any man especially a husband, what are you talking about? I am just fine I love just being your wife and you my man and I have a friend if I am lonely I got someone to pray with, talk with, go to dinner with, and to yell at, I laugh because I had always talked to God like he was and is my best friend since I develop a relationship with him. This was the end of 2005, I ignored the voice of God because I was so happy with my life in Jesus, I did not want to anything to interfere with the love I had for God, this guy ministry was singing at this church at the time and I was walking out the door and the spirit of God spoke again saying go and give him a kiss on the check for me and let him know that I love him, and it will be okay, I said to myself lord are you okay? I will not touch that man, he would think I want him and I am okay, then the lord ask me if you love me and obey me like you say then you would trust what I am saying, I was kind of mad, but I obeyed the voice of God I walked back into the church and walked over to the young man and gave him a hug and kissed him on the cheek and told him that God loves him and it will be okay, he looked at me with a surprise, with a smile like he knew what I was saying was true, he said thank you and I went on my way, I kind of laughed to myself and said lord you are off the hook. At this time I went home and me and my mother was talking about some things in my past, my mother never wanted to hear about the past she was getting upset and did not want to deal with what she did or cause, so I just prayed that God would let her know that she got to face some things before God could release her to her future.

Some thing she was in denial in, she knew it was true, but she wanted to leave it behind with out forgiving or ask for forgiveness, so I started taking her to the church I was going to and she loved it she started seeing the spirit of God move in people life's, then she started getting involved and in 2006 she gave her life to Christ. Even through she gave her life it still was some things God needed her to do in her, she still had something in her that hinder her from loving me totally. Well me and this man I meet in church started to communicate more that I met, and everything was not that great in this man all he ever did was jump from woman to woman and he was a good man deep down inside, and we had a lot in common, but I had to go to God and say lord I know you don't have this man for me because he got to much work that need to be done in him for me to deal with, but we became best friends, I would talk to him a lot concerning my struggles and he would open up to me concerning his, it was hard to really date, him but we was friends because of his life style with to many other women that I would put a red flag up, but I would always encourage him to read his word and let God love him the way he need to be love, we really had a lot in common, his loneliness and wanted to be love and some one to love him, I remember when I felt that way, our back ground was kind of the same but he was raised with his parent and he was not abused, but he did feel not supported to become a success in his life, but I would encourage him with my testimony to let him know it was never to late for God to change and arrange him in what God is calling him to be. A Godly man first. That man had a good heart it was just all over the place, but some reason God connected us together I just did not see my self-being his wife, at least at that time. But we enjoyed each other company, well now It is 2007 and my mother is still holding on still fighting this sickness she has in and out of hospitals and nursing home, I prayed everyday that God would bless her, we started spending more time like a mother and daughter should, I loved my mother, we had some ups and down but our relationship became stronger, even with all her hurt she afflicted me with, I found myself loving her through it all. I had a great help in dealing with what I was going through, a mother of the church that had twelve boys told me no matter what we go through or what people have done to us we got to have a different approach, we got to give as children of God, we only would have one mother no matter how many play a role as a mother God gave us our parents and to respect and show love just toward the blessing in that, it made me think that no matter what happen I got through because of the seed God implant me within, and maybe something happened in my mother past that cost her traumas that intervene in caring for me, and some generational curses are to be broken and not mended back together, my mother started being a friend to me even with the hidden backstabbing at this time, I really did not care I just wanted to love her and forgive her and be the daughter she needed me to be. I really would not understand her pain, only God! I don't know what she has been through. But I was here for her incase she wanted to open up; I just wanted her to know that she was forgiven and I loved her no matter what.

So this brother and me started dating trying a relationship he was singing for God and I was called to preach and teach his word, we became closer as time went by, he helped me a lot in caring for my mother, but there was always some type of issue he had, woman! Because I was saving myself for God right time in for my life, he did not totally understand that because of the women he dated allowed him to stay and live and sleep with them, and these women were in church like I was, but as time went by I explain to him some of my past so he could understand, I gave him scriptures to look up so he would understand the temple of God, I hated to see him in this type of web that the devil was holding him in so I prayed for his deliverance, I asked God why the man I was friends with for four years never tried or ask to touch me and we spent lots and more time together than the man you say would be my husband? One preaches the word and they other sang the word? But as time went by I understood that the enemy had deceived him so many times and all he ever wanted was love and God was the one that was going to give it to him and I needed to be patient and see the salvation of God move. Sometime we give up on people before God tells us to and a lot of us miss out on our true blessings. The funny thing about being with him he hurt him to even hear that I went through the things I went through and his heart was so much in making me happy pleasing me talking to me like the lord would have some do but I rejected it a lot because of his short coming of wanting me to love him not only mentally but physically to and I was not to take it to that level, but we remained good friends through it all I was always busty and in and out of town working for the lord, to tell you the truth I never had a man that shared tears with me and cared that much about what happen to me even my friend from church did not do that so I knew he had some form of God in him, he just did not know how to really let go and let God work it out for him, he did not know about the holy spirit that comes in and live in you the power he needed to change some things in him. No one ever took the time to explain or teach him what the word of God says about this type of activity. So the devil knew his weakness and tried to destroy him with it, but we know God is always on time. Well it is 2007 still hanging in there with mom and this new love I got in my life but still depending on God for what I need and want, ministry was strong it had its ups and down, but we know that everyone that call On the name can also be full of game, the lord was using me in ways I never could of imagine, my life testimony helped a lot of people and the relationships, what I had with my mom, helped delivered other daughters and mothers. At this time I was going through a lot my mother had truly turned to the worst, her health had put her in intensive care and I was so busy running back and fourth to the hospital, not knowing but holding on to faith that God would pull her through I needed a little more time with my mother. It still was things I needed to talk to her about, and at this time I did get a little weak in my walk with God, my man friend was going through some things so we feed off each other strength, I allowed him to move in to help him out for awhile at this time, I felt that I was doing the right thing I hated to see anyone in need, like I used to be. And if I had it I would share to the world no matter who it was.

But my spirit was warning me and I just did not believe I would fall to temptation. I felted strong enough in the lord to sustain myself from any temptation, so I thought.

But who was I fooling we were sharing to much time together, then the kissing came from time to time then the hugging and the love taps, lord help me please! I never felt the feelings I felt with him, I thought I was safe. Finally I could not contain myself, he started telling me that he wanted to spend the rest of his life with me and he needed a woman like me and I remember that God said that this man was going to be my husband, and I just let all the guard I had down, I never had a man that stayed home at night cooked, cleaned ran my bath water, loved kids, listened to me, I just thought well lord forgive me even though the love making was good, but what happen to God commandments, I felt like I just died I never wanted to let God down again, I really wanted to make it until the time was right. I did not save myself for my husband. I was celibate for seven years! Never been touched by anyone, I felt that I was heading for a disaster. So I cried out to God to please forgive me I wanted to be different for once in my life, I felt guilty, I felt dirty, then I punished myself, asking myself how I allow myself to fall so short of your glory? Was I really weak? Was I really in the will of God? Was I really your chosen vessel lord? How did I allow myself to give in so easily? How could I listen to the enemy and let him trick me? The list went on and on. I wanted my man friend to know that I was special would he look at me the same? Or as the other women he had before? How could or would he treat me different from them? We had some thing special and I messed it all up! I was the stronger vessel, how could I fall Lord? This was all I thought about, I let God down, myself down, my man friend down, I had let too much of myself out and gave to soon. But he did not leave he wanted to work it out he wanted me to teach him how to love me but only God could do that. So after the fall I prayed and talk with God to help us both get it right, he made me feel so safe like no man could ever do, he stayed until we got married June 14, 2008, and believe me the devil tried us both up to that day, to separate us, my mind was playing tricks on me all the time, had me believing it was not to be, but I held on to what God said and did not care what every one else thought, it was so sad that everyone else knows what is good for you, but not for themselves, at times I thought that he was not for me because of the arguing and other people in our life's, but I took a long hard look at what was going on, and talked to God and I knew that he was not ready to be a husband because God was not done with him yet, not that he was not my husband, the lord let me know that in the beginning we just jumped before our season but know instead of blaming one another, we needed to come together and allow God to bring the season to us by reading our word together, praying together, going to church together, fellowshipping ourselves with other couples that are growing together, take our relation to God not people, hold each other up when one fall, and look at our own faults instead of blaming one another, and allow God to be the leader the middle and the end of our marriage. We might have got married for all the wrong reason but I rather marry than to burn the word tells us in Corinthians: chapter seven verse nine tells us if they cannot contain, let them marry; for it is better to Marry than to burn, when I gave myself to a man, it made me feel that I gave the my most precious thing that God had for me to preserve, and I let him down, it is so sad how we allow ourselves to be caught up in this judgmental world of what people would think of you, or look down on you.

So I allow myself to be caught up with this title I had trying not to let anyone know that I made a mistake, but God knew, and that was all I needed to worry about not man judgment on my life, but to tell you the truth I am happy being married looking for the end of what God have for us just the guilt was eating me up, and keeping me from totally given in to my husband and looking at all the faults he had before we got married. It was nothing new that he did or said, I just let myself be caught up with the rumors of what people thought of him, or his past, but every thing he did I knew before I married him. So now I am putting this marriage before God and waiting on his change and movement in changing him and me, but the more I had put my marriage before God the more the enemy fought against it, it had got so bad with my mother playing a part, jealous people playing a part, I started to change, I started loosing who I was in God, my drive I had for God, I lost my peace I had with God, I lost my passion for the ministry God had in me, I starting loosing the most important thing my relationship with God, it seemed like my past was knocking at the door and it seemed like it had keys to come in to take my mind. I knew that the devil is a liar, I knew that my marriage was not a joke, it was God that spoke to me to let me know, it was me that did not wait on the right time, I was so angry of being the strong one in the marriage I wanted my husband to take control for once but I was to scared to give him that chance, so I hid the pain again until it ate like cancer, my whole house hold was in chaos and I needed God to take control, at this time, I really did not trust the women or men in the church for advice because of what they would tell me, that man is not your husband, because of his action, but never offered to help him to understand what was at stack! At this time I knew my husband was not strong spiritually but he was Gods child and he just needed a male model in the spiritual family to lead him in the right direction not for them to throw stones and bury him, so I started taking my scream I had inside out on him, not that he did not deserve it some of the times, but it was not my battle to fight it was the lord, one day I screamed at God and told him I need you now if nothing else change around me then change me. Not that I deserve anything because of my disobedience, but because lord I need you now this is to big for me to handle, then here we are 2009 and my mother had to go back to the hospital I was so drained and tiered I just could not move another step my marriage was messed up, the devil seem to be winning at this point, and I just did not care if I would live to see it through another day. Because I did not care to pray read or go to church, I know this sounds like De'javo all over again, this is when I realize that Satan has no new tricks he will bring the same trick your past sins to you in all types of different forms, we just got to recognize the pattern, and any thing else we do to our selves God always give you a sign on when, where and how your destruction will come. we just got to stop and truly listen and stop wanting to please the flesh all the time, if you was training for a job you would follow instructions and finish the probation period, If you meet a new woman or man you was dating you would put on every thing positive to make sure that this person would like you, if you was meeting the president for the very first time How would your approach be? Then all the preparations that you would do for worldly things then what would you do for the lord? And how would you follow the instructions when the lord tells you?

If only we would stop, listen, relate, pay attention and follow the voice of the lord, a lot of turmoil we go through would not be so bad, we would see the victory shout at the end of every tunnel. When I started getting tired of being tired of being just to tired, this is when I straighten my self up and said to my self girl you got what it takes, God has brought you to far for you to keep going in circles, when are you going to pay attention and go straight, I was My own worst enemy, because every time that I would fall I would look back and reach into my own past that the lord had deliver me from, it was only there to remind me of how I made it through, it was only there for me to testify about, and to glorify the lord of how good he is to me, it was only there for me to know that I am his chosen vessel, but I kept on reaching for it to be a covering, an excuse for me to through my pity parties all over again. I was stopping my self from a lot of doors opening and closing, I had my hand in the situation more than God; the lord did not choose me to fail, but to succeed the entire plan he had for me. To prosper and not to fail, We got to stop planning where we are going in God and just follow the plan in the order that is already ordain for our life, we get of focus to much because of self, we always want things, people and places faster than God has for us, something's are like playing hot potatoes, it is to hot to handle at that time and God wants to cool it down for us to handle. But we always in a rush and with out patience, in his word Jeremiah he say this, just as plain as you can read, for I know the Plan I have for you, Declares the Lord' Plans to Prosper you and not to Harm you, Plans to give you Hope and a Future, and in Isaiah 40 verse 31, But they that wait on the lord shall Renew their strength; they shall mount up with wings as eagles; they shall run and not be weary; and they shall walk and not faint. Now tell me if we believe that he died for us, so that we can live, then why is it so hard to know that God has it all covered? Because it was all a " Set Up" for his plan to work, that he already had just for us, yes we can shed our tears but know that in Psalm chapter 30 verse five the lord speaks about his anger only endures but a moment in his favor is life so our weeping may endue for a night, but joy comes in the morning, I have falling so many times on God, my faith, my joy, my peace, my happiness, my hope, my plan, my purpose, and my belief, but when I thought about the goodness of Jesus and all that he has done for me I said girl you are tripping, get up pick back up that cross, and start the walking all over again, you are a solider of the most high God, and what you have and is going through is only a test of your faith being awake while you rest! You are more than a conquerors though Christ that love you, and I shall live and not die. Said the lord! I had to get my self back in order no matter what was going on all around me, my marriage was falling apart, my kids were acting like fools, my spiritual family was lacking in encouraging me, so I had to encourage my self, by reading my word, fasting and praying and having hope that my change was on the way. Now it had came that may mom was leaving me, we still have not resolved all my answers, I still was puzzled to know if she truly loved me or not, but I thank God I had the time of having her in my life, we had built a relation ship some was good and some was bad, but tell me who has a perfect relationship? I got what I needed and that was my mother again, to hold and kiss her, and to tell her that I loved her, not only that but to show her that in spit of what, how, or who said what God had done this thing, and he was in charge.

I was able to let go and let God heal a broken piece in me that I never had fix and that was a time with my mother, and to truly forgive her, my mother past away to be with the lord on July the 3 2009, I never knew that it was going to be that hard to let go, because we only had a little time together but I know that I had the time and I had to give God the thanks for that, I felt like apart of me was gone, I felt so bad for my baby sister because she was in prison when our mother past away, and I wanted to be there for her, and I couldn't, I knew that she depend on my mother for everything and it was going to be bad for her to let go. I was blaming myself for not having my mother in my home at the time she died she had gotten so sick that it was so hard for me alone to care for her, and I had so much going on in my marriage that I did not want her to suffer no more than she already was, I picked her up one day from the nursing home she had been in there 2 weeks, and for some reason I felt that me and her needed to have lunch together, and spend this day together, so I brought her back home and fix lunch for us both and we had the best time we ever had through my whole life together that is, she had told me that she knew that I had been through a lot, and that she was so sorry that I went through all that pain, she open up to me about some things that had happened to her in her child hood of her being raped and beating, and her street life, tears were in my eyes to know I finally got the answer I needed my mother had gone through some pain like I had and no one helped her or loved her the way she needed to be loved, until she came here and received Christ in her life. She thanked me for everything I did and told me she was sorry and really want me to be happy, she could not eat the lunch I fix, and became very tired and wanted to go back to the nursing home and lay down. I never knew that it was our last supper together; the next day I got a call that my mother was not Responding and they were sending her to the hospital when I got there she was not looking good, I was so full of pain and really had no one there for me but God, so I cried out to the lord asking him to please take her pain away let her not suffer any more, no matter what it cost me, give her rest, I came home and told my husband after I got out the shower before I was going back to the hospital that God was going to take my mother, I went back to the hospital the doctors let me know that she was not doing good, and that they were not able to get her mediation in her, So the last two days I had with her was just me letting her know that I love her and forgive her, as I laid in the bed with her and holding her hand I told her that I would be okay, and she can rest with God now, with tears in my eyes I did not want to let go now we just stared talking to one another and opening up to one another, I felt that I needed more time with her, but I needed to let go and let God do what he needed to do for her sake, my mother was a energizer bunny always on the go and shopping and doing her favorite dance. She opened her eyes for a minute and called my name, as I was standing she called with a loud voice, I will never forget the loud sound she made, like she wants me to be okay and did not want to leave me again, until I was okay but I let her know that I was okay, and that God had me. I told her that I will and shall be happy, and that she can let go now. I gave her a kiss told her I would be right back I went home and asked my husband to come to the hospital with me because my mom was not doing well, and I need someone with me, I truly knew that this was it and I was going to say good bye to my Mom.

I was gone for only fifteen minutes, when I walked in her room I seen a tear in her eye, and walked toward her, at that second she looked at me walking in the hospital room, and then when I got closer to her she stop breathing, she had waited on me to return before she let go and went with God, lord it hurt more than I ever could of imagine. Then my mother phone rang and it was my baby sister on the phone and I had to let her know that our mother just past, that was the worst news I wanted to give her while she was locked up, all I could do is say lord help her and give her strength. As I was dealing with all this my heart was so heavy no one around me really truly knew what I was feeling because all they knew was my mother never raised me, so it should not be hard but they really did not and cannot understand the deep hidden love I had for my mother, a love that God planted and no matter what people thought and seen, she was my mother. And I loved her. I was so hard on myself because my mother never wanted to go in a nursing home but at the last days I had to, I was going through to much I wanted to leave my marriage, things were not good at all, so I started to blame myself for her dieing early, so as I was planning the homecoming service for my mother I was sitting in my chair with tears in my eyes wondering lord I don't know how I am going to pay for my mother funeral her insurance was not much, I just got it when she moved from New York and I had to have it over two years and it was only 19 months that I had it, so I was crying and I heard a voice call out my name it was so plain that everyone in the house could of heard it, so I got up walked to my bedroom and asked my husband did he call me, he said no so I went back and sat In the chair and the voice called me again I said to my husband I know you called me, and he responded you are tripping, I did not call you then I said to myself girl you are tripping, you better call on Jesus, I looked at my mothers picture and said ok mom what are we going to do? Letting her know that I was sorry for putting her in the nursing home, I told her that I was sorry for not being able to care for her myself and keep her home, because of all the arguing, I did not want her to get sick any more and I was sorry for her seeing me act a fool, every now and then, being a woman of God I should have had better control, even through me and you had our ups and down I needed you to stay focus on God so he could heal your body, I was talking to her picture like I she was standing their herself in the flesh. I was so angry with my husband for not helping the situation get better, I was mad that he was not a strong vessel at the time of my weakness, I felt like I was in this marriage alone and fighting for a lost battle. At that moment I felt a calm hand go across my face I looked around to see if anyone touched me, that Touch was a mother touch, I know that touch it felt like that the touch that my mother gave me on my wedding day, at the moment I could not stop crying I knew that my mother heard me and knew that I loved her and she was watching over me. And that she was okay, it was just too hard to say goodbye for now. Now it was two weeks after my mother was gone I was going through some personal feelings inside and needed God to help me understand something's, maybe I was not reaching out to God enough, being so weak and the church family did not check on me since the funeral, and that was so sad when you think you got the people of God to help you through a difficult time it was no one around, so I took out some of the pain I was feeling on my husband, because of what I had went through with my him, the things he had done and allowed the enemy to step in and direct him in a mess up state of mind, I was mad that he did not feel the pain I was feeling and the abandonment I was feeling so instead Of forgiving and working it out I wanted to push him further away from me, I slow down the women ministry, it seemed like all it was doing was sucking more life out of me, I let go of the children ministry, I did not have enough drive to push myself to gather them together, I was tired of going to church with the same old testimonies and songs and people acting like they cared, but when you leave you don't get a card or call or not even a knock on the door, so I separated myself, from forms of things, but not God, I loved the lord no matter what I was feeling, I knew with out a shadow of any doubt he loved me and cared for me, I talk to the lord daily, I was driving my car one day and heard the lord voices asking me why have you looked for others to wipe the tears away? Why are you looking in all the wrong places? I am here with you I will give you the strength you need just ask, you are forgiven, forgive yourself, I have set you free from all the fruit from the bad tree, I have planted a new seed in you that wants to bare the good fruit, that I have being watering in you, but the branches are growing but the weeds that you picked up are in the way of keeping the good fruit from blooming, just step aside and let me finish the good work I have started in you. And when I stepped aside and let go and let God, he started plucking the weeds, and now I was feeling my fruit grow! The tears that I have been shedding night and day since my youth has build me a harvest that is waiting for me, this is when I received that key to endue the tears I was shedding through my walk with God, I had receive the power to stand through any test that has and is coming my way, I am God's anointed I am chosen, Glory be to God, when I was able to stop my car I jumped out and did a victory dance it was like fire shut up in my bones, I felt like David in the bible, I danced so hard my clothes almost came off, I was finally free from my own self destruction do this mean I am perfect? And will not go through any thing else? Or that my trails and tribulations were over? No it means to me that I am who God says I am, I belong to him, and I will make it, no matter what storms, winds, floods, hurricanes, tornadoes, come my way as long as I got king Jesus I can make it. And believe me the devil is not done I am a threat to his mess, for one I love the lord, second I got the lord in me, third I am obeying the lord word, fourth I am following the lord, fifth I got a made up mind, six I have gotten back up from the traps he set for me to fall, and seven I got the power to resist him when he appears. One day I was at home and going through some things of my mothers, looking throw all her paper work and clothes and packing things up to save for my sister and I run across a tablet, I open it up and it was a journal, that my mother was keeping it was her last words I never knew she was writing, and it was all about me how she loved me how I was her angel, how she was so proud of me, how she thank God for having me, and how she was so proud and happy that she was with me at her last days, it was touching I cried through reading it all, I had my answer, Thank you Lord my Mother really did love me and never wanted to give me away, she was trapped by the enemy games just like I was, and was glad that I was the one who rescued her. Thank you Jesus I have peace.

Now it is September 2009 I am at home and my phone rings, I get a call that my Son is very ill and I need to get up to the hospital, I was a little caught off guard because we just buried my mother and My husband nephew got shoot a few months back multiple times and almost lost his life, so we were very busy in 2009 things were coming back to back, but thank God for his grace and mercy. So I got up out of my bed rushed to the hospital and there it was another attack from the enemy to take me off course, of what I just got delivered from, yes I was scared, yes I was hurt, yes I screamed, and yes I cried, I am still human and God gave me this heart, all I was getting from the doctors were your son is very critical and he will not make it through the night, he has an infection that went through his whole body and into his heart that broke pieces of his heart that went into his brain that caused him three massive strokes, and if we do surgery or cut on him now he will die, all I could do is take a deep breath, and did my motherly cry and scream and panic, and then shook myself and said okay that enough now God I am here again and you know what I am going through, you knew before it ever happened, so tell me lord and only you tell me the real deal, I had a long talk with you lord and you told me if I step aside and let you be the lord you need to be in my life, then you would care for my every need and some of my wants, now lord I want you to fix this, I needed you to strengthen me and carry me through what ever you got planned. This situation is to deep and close to my heart, and it is a heavy load that I can not bear to carry, heal my son right now lord, raise him up lord like you did me lord, I know your miracles lord! When you raised Lazarus up lord, how you healed the blind and deaf, how you made the woman with the issue of blood whole, now do it for my son lord, in the name of Jesus, this was the first step I took to allow God to wipe my tears, not my husband, not my pastor, not my daughter, not my son, not my friends, but God. This is when I saw some weeds moving that was stopping my victory, and when I allowed myself to depend totally on God and trust him at his word, he told me first that my son was going to be okay and then he sent a pastor that told me everything was going to be okay, and the another pastor that was the Father the Son and the Holy Ghost that confirmed that my son will live again! With a new clean heart. Thank you Jesus you are bad all by your self, my husband was not there by my side, I was upset that he was not holding me through this time, that was very trying, but I thank God he was not because this help me depend on God totally, this was my test of faith, to see how I was going to deal with this, even my daughter could not make it here, she had relocated and was living in Atlanta and my baby boy was over seas and no one was able to be here for me at that moment, it seemed like God moved everyone so I could show him that I truly believed him at his word and to show me that he was and is the only one that can wipe my tears away! So they did the heart surgery and replaced the heart vale in his heart, he had to be on three different antibiotics but God is good and bad all by him self, I had separated from my husband a few times doing our marriage to be able to really hear from the lord before I decided to walk away the marriage, because the enemy was having his way, because we both was not doing what we needed to do and that was pray together, read the word together, hold each other up, and resist all temptations I could blame him and he could blame me but all in all we should of look at ourselves, I had no excuse.

Everyone around me was trying to tell me what was best for me, and what God said, this is what happens when you let people into your marriage instead of God. The only middleman that can fix any problem and it comes out the way God say it should is God himself, anything else will tear it apart. So this last time that we split up was a good one

God spoke to us both, I confessed my faults to the lord and admitted to myself that Rome never was built in a day, and it takes patience for God to move, I know with out a shadow of a doubt that this was my husband we were brought together for a reason but we rushed our season, so we got to wait until the hand on God clock reach the time we rushed. You see you can mess up your own destiny by allowing the flesh to go before the spirit like I did, but you got to recognize the mistake and stop blaming everything, and everyone else, that seems to be easy to point the blame, even only we stop look and evaluate the problem. I let sin in before the blessing, I allowed dedication before education, the call we both had was perfect in God eyes but we allowed the lack of the our knowledge come before the change, we knew each other in the flesh but not in the spirit, we both had the right key but it was not molded yet to fit in the right lock, we had use our spiritual walk unwisely, but I am ready do what I need to do to get it right, there is a firm foundation that the lord has for us to stand on and the enemy has a quick sand for us to step in. and no matter how God shows, tells or warns us, we just got to have it our way, the lord is not a restaurant, that you can order only what you like. You got to eat the whole meal when God prepares something for you, and that was what we were lacking some one forgot the vegetables or did not eat the meat we both jumped to the desert, We always follow our plan, and then when it don't work we look at God like he never played the movie for us, he gave it to us for free, but we just had to go pay for someone else copy. And we did not pay attention on what he really had on the inside, to see how much it really was going to cost us. Me and my husband was separated three times never stayed away to long but long enough to see that we Did this, no one forced us, we agreed before God to do this no matter if it was now or later, so now we got A little more struggles to endue, long as we let go and let God show us his way and his plan and his wisdom and knowledge we would be able to understand why we got to go through to receive. Now we are together holding on to see what God had in the beginning, when we stop looking through other people eyes because it looks and seem bad but look through Gods eyes and see the hidden treasures then we know with out a shadow of any doubt that God has called for this to be, we just did it before his time, so we got to just wait on the lord and his will for us, Thank you Jesus I can't wait to see the results. Take a cake when you bake it do you share it before it gets Done? Or do you wait until it is finished and cool off, before you cut a piece? That's like God he wants to finish the project enough to present it to you, and that way when a piece falls, it would not be difficult to pick it up and place it back in the right place. Allow what ever you do for God be of good timing and in the right season before you drive off, stop when the light is red, yield when the caution light is flashing and go when it turns green.

No I am not finished, and yes my marriage will and is a working process, but when God gets finish then we know it is time to leave this earth. No matter what it is that you have or doing with God never give up until God say so, because every thing that serves God is a working process and will not be totally finish until he comes back for us, but you will see good results up until that appointed day we have with him. I have other things that are going to come my way, but I am ready and getting ready to move to the next level so watch out haters of the world, I am coming out and I want the world to know what God is going to show, in me, through me, and around me, so what ever the devil thought he has done, God is working it out in my favor, Psalm sixty eight verse one says let God arise, let his enemies be scattered; let them also that hate him flee before him, as smoke is driven away, so drive them away as wax melt, before the fire, so let the wicked perish at the presence of God! It is sad that people would bet and sit around just to see what's going on in your life, always wondering what is the next moved, but when I was a little girl no one cared what was going on never wanted to hear the pain, but loved to see you play the game of failure, they would follow my life when I would go left, they would follow my life when I would go right, they even followed my life when I went backwards and especially when I felled, but when I got up and went straight they would not follow any more. What a laugh I love it!! Thank you Jesus, I asked the lord one day, lord what do you have on my life that when I walk the ground shakes? I thank God every day I want to see what my ends going to be. It is not easy being chosen, being called is like walking through, but being chosen is going through, we have came to far with to much testimony to turn back now, I don't like to test a lie, but I want to share that God is able to make it work if we put it in his hands, so I guess you are wondering if my tears have been wiped away yet? No but they have been getting lighter and lighter as the trails and tribulations comes, me and my husband decided that we are not to old that God can't bless look at Abraham and Sarah, we are still together even through it has not been that long, but rather it is one year or fifty years we made a vow to the lord to allow him to do what he needs to do with us, so hang on and see how the next book of my story ends, don't forget God is making us over and it takes time, that only the lord knows. If God can't do it, no one can. I thank the lord for not letting me go, and helping me to understanding the battle that he has won on my behalf, no matter what the world throws God has a mitt that can caught all things on your behalf. Let me share a little something with you, When I thought that it was all over for my marriage I called a divorce attorney and paid the money and when it was time to sign I was at the social security office and a stranger sat next to me, we sat for a while, I never had met her before in my life, then she spoke and told me that God said not to get rid of my marriage, he was going to work it out, I was mad but for a moment, but glad that I obeyed the lord even when the tear I had was to big for me, God sent an angel unaware to wipe that tear, so now I know that it is not over until the lord has spoken. Sometimes we need to encourage ourselves, in the word of God and know that God is still on the throne of his promise.

Through the good and the bad, know that the battle is already Won through Jesus Christ, this is my Christmas gift to the lord the sacrifice of letting go of the past by Sharing my story to the world, it is December 2009 and I am still holding on to the promises of God, no it is still a battle, and still a walk I got to go, but I know now that what ever I go through at this point God got it, if I would give it to him, I have a choice to walk the way he is showing me or follow someone else or do it my self, it is up to me, if I want to stay a winner by doing what's right, humble myself under subjection to the spirit of God, I can allow the lord to take me to heaven or I can put myself in hell! I truly thank the lord for giving me the courage and strength to come out the hidden closet, to share not only my story, but the testimony of my life story, there will be more coming but know I am not that little girl any more that was looking for everyone and every thing to wipe my tears away, I know now that when it is all over I know who is the lord of all my joy and who is going to wipe all the tears away, he let me know in Revelation chapter 21 verse 3 through seven, it says this and I heard a great voice out of heaven saying,

Behold, the tabernacle of God is with men, and he will dwell with them. And they shall be his people, and God himself shall be with them, and be their God. And God shall wipe away all tears from their eyes; and there shall be no more death. Neither sorrow, nor crying, neither shall there be any more pain: for the former things are passes away. And he said unto me, it is done. I am Alpha and Omega the beginning and the end. I will give unto him that is athirst of the fountain of the water of life freely. He that overcomes shall inherit all things and I will be his God, and he shall be my son. After reading this all I could do is shout and know that the tears were temporary it was all for my good to mold me into what I need to be and become today and I still am being worked on but with a better drive to know what my out come is going to be great, if I continue holding on to the lords word. I am trying to reach all of God's people that are full of sorrow, pain, depression, loneliness, abuse, neglect, abandoned, and shame, to let them know that God is the tear of Joy. And his word is life! It is true, oh yes it is, just pick it up read, believe and receive and look at me I am one of his witnesses, read all about yourself, one day I heard a pastor talk about the keys to the kingdom of God, and I made a comment that the word of God the bible is our keys to one and only true love of our life, and as I read the lord words daily I see myself in a lot of the women in the bible. The lord would show you what you need to know if you just get out of that self pity the enemy has trap you in, like myself and get the strength you need to come out of them dark deep places that no one was ever able to reach it is so sad to be in church getting up daily Sundays after Sunday and bible studies and lie to yourself that you learn something or you got delivered but still have no forgiveness toward anyone that hurt you, or to hold on to giving because someone always took advantaged of you, or to smile to leave and have that same frown when the doors shut. We have mothers, sisters, brothers, aunts, uncles, fathers, cousins and even friends that we don't help because of that unforgiving deep down spirits that has not come out yet, that is hindering you from your purpose, the destiny God is trying to bring you to.

I hope as I share some of these women in the bible to you, that you would see yourself in them, and just shout and know that it is okay, God got your back' just let him know that you need his covering; it will cost you nothing that you did not need in the beginning. This book is for all of Gods children even a man yes a man. Because in the beginning God created man and then made female from mans rib so that one day we will be able to become one in wholeness of the spirit of God that dwells in us and we will be able to touch in agreement.

These are the women in the bible God had given me that was in my childhood through my Adult hood.

1. Tamar who was violated by family member from the spirit of lust and was discarded, after being used by the enemy by the grief of the shame and no one wanting to believe as a child so we felt no escape of the violence we began hatred into our hearts because no one done nothing to help, so here it is a lifelong emotional trauma so hear we are feeling like Tamar the fear, the pain, and shame of being raped and violated by someone you trust.

2. Hagar: the spirit of being rejected, abandoned and low self esteem Satan would make you feel that you are in danger to yourself he would try to destroy you before you know your purpose, even before you find the destiny that the lord has plan for you making you feel that you are bad person, never going to be nothing no one want you, you have no right to the tree of life, and that you never going to be anything thing because no one would love you because you are surrogate mother,

3. Beersheba: a woman of beauty only by body being married and having lust after another man, desire of the flesh, and trick by the devil that would cause death and the enemy set up a death trap for someone you love allowing Satan to damage the good before God could work it out for us.

4. Women with the Issue of Blood: she had suffered for twelve long years with a disease of the issues of blood no one wanted her to touch them all her procession and money was spent on doctors that made her to believe that she was dome until she heard about a man name Jesus that would and could heal her and make her whole so she pushed her way through and got her healing and

that is what some of us need to do push our way through no matter what any one say the doctors, the lawyers, our friends, family members, or our enemies we got someone that can heal all issues of life and the blood is what he healed us with.

5. Samaritan Women a social outcast: it was about her having to many husbands and the one that she had was not her own and this made her an outcast some one with an embarrassing situation with different men in her life that people would only talk about instead help and teach her the right way.

6. Leah: the unwanted wife a person that was given and not chosen out of age and duty she had to become someone wife that wanted someone else. So his love for was not real in the beginning had to grow out of duty.

7. Now a person that we all need and wanted to be label as a Virtuous Woman: a woman that every one could be proud of, a rare woman that first fear and reverenced God and righteousness a crown to her husband and far more than rubies to her children all would be proud of.

In these seven characters that God let me learn about, I have seen myself as having and developing the same a person all in me, so allow me to go through all of them again, only the name of the character is was I!

1. I was violated by my family members I was made to be a piece of flesh for them to do what ever and when even they wanted to use me, I was discarded after the enemy had his way, by the grief of shame that this happened no one ever believing me as a child, I felt no escape, this had me developing more hatred in my heart because not having a mother to talk to about this, and if I had someone would they done anything? It was a lifelong emotional trauma for me, and I felt just like Tamar full of fear, pain, and shame, of being molested by someone you are suppose to trust. But the lord has shown me the love, understanding,

and compassion God shown me that he was all the comfort I ever needed, to start my healing, he taught me how to forgive myself and others, in Psalms chapter twenty seven verse ten when my mother and father forsake me, then the lord will take me up. And in Isaiah chapter forty one verse ten, eleven, and thirteen it says fear not for I am with you, be not dismayed, for I am you God; I will strengthen you, I will help you, I will lift you with my righteousness. Behold, all that are incensed against me shall be ashamed and confounded for the lord my God will hold me saying fear not: and believe me the lord is helping me every day of my life by guarding my heart and my mind by keeping it in perfect peace.

2. I was feeling rejected and feeling abandoned by every one I ever came in contact with, I allow Satan to make me believe that my plan for my life was always going to be danger, I felt that if I reached out I would be destroyed even if I tried. I never felt that I had a destiny but failure, so he planted surrogates mothers in my life to make be believe I would never know a love from my real natural mother, I felt like I was a bad person, and never going to be anything in life, by being a foster child that made me have low self esteem, the enemy tried to make me feel that I had no rights to the tree of life. But the lord let me know that I was precious and wanted if I would just allow him to come in and give me what was missing in my life, and live again, he let me know that I was born again, a new creature and I would be rejected for righteousness and his name sake.

3. I felt like my body was my only beauty, the lust of the flesh was all I had to give, I was married and living with another man, because of me never hear that I was beautiful I allowed the words from men to lead me in a death situation, he lust of the eyes can be a trick to your destiny, beauty is what God has created and not what man made, we need to watch out for the sweet talkers dressed in sheep clothing, know that we need to be a bride for Jesus before we can be wife or husbands for others. Know that God has the keys to repair and restore, confession

is good for the soul, Psalm chapter fifty one verse one and two, have mercy upon me, O God according to thy loving kindness; according unto the multitude of thy tender mercies blot out my transgressions wash me thoroughly from mine iniquity, and cleanse me from sins and one John chapter verse eight and nine if we say that we have no sin, we deceive ourselves, and the truth is not in us, if we confess our sins, he is faithful and just to forgive us of our sins,

4. After reading my story you know that I have suffered many issues that held me from being washed in the Blood of Jesus Christ, just being afflicted with all that man said I had, I truly thank the lord for the faith That he had build up in me, when every thing had me feeling like I was dome God gave me hope, everything that the enemy was and is bringing my way he had to get permission from God to even attack, but as long as I hold onto the hem of his garment the word I will and shall be made whole in the lord, in Matthew chapter nine verse twenty one and twenty two, let me know that if I would just touch the hem of his garment and believe that he is who he say he is by faith it would make be whole again, so matter what people think or say concerning my life I know that if I keep on pushing my way through the mess, the chaos, the backbiting, the lies, the close doors, in Matthew chapter seventeen verse twenty tells me a grain of a mustard seed of faith we can move the mountains in our life and know that we walk by faith and not by sight.

Things might look bad and it seen like you will not make it through, it's only the circumstances'

God is the result.

I have made so many mistake in my life and still today and tomorrows I will make them, and their

Will be saints that really are aints that will try to keep you down by them mistakes, but keep getting up, try your best, give God your reasonable service, yourself daily, you would always be a outcast to them that don't understand the calling on your life, it hard for you to understand but the battle is not with my brothers or sisters or myself it got nothing to do with me it was all about Jesus so keep your head up I had to tell myself over and over again I am just a vessel being use by God that is awesome all by itself. There will be haters wondering why and how you walked out that fire you were just thrown in, how did God give her another and another and another chance why is because I got up and carry the cross that was meant for me. Then wipe the dust off your shoulders and keep on walking. Still drinking from the fountain of life his cup the word, my life.

No matter how hard I tried to please the man in my life rather he was a friend or my husband, if they were not a man from God, than you would still be trying to please the flesh, they would always want something to keep pleasing them flesh is never satisfy, so if you can't please God! Then why try pleasing Man? The eyes of the flesh seeks all that would keep it please, no matter how much I tried to be a model wife my buttons always got stuck and then I was cast aside but no matter how much your button breaks or stick God got the right tool to make it work so now I put all my love and energy in the lord to mold me into what he wants me to be, you cannot give what you can't give to God, Exodus Chapter twenty verse three tells us not to bow down to men or serve them for God is our God and a Jealous God so how can we worship man more than our creator? I was Leah a unwanted wife because I allowed others to seek out the person for me and God did chose that husband for me, that is what we do today we allow someone else to tell us that is our husbands or we go out seeking ourselves, when in Proverbs chapter eighteen verse twenty two tells us whosoever finds a wife finds a good thing, and obtain favor of the lord God will send the husband in good timing his time so that we would receive the love, support, devotion, compassion, we need to become a wanted wife.

Last and the best that I am still striving for to become for my lord and Savior Jesus Christ and to my husband, and myself is a "Virtuous Woman," a person that is hard to find a woman that totally fears the lord, she takes her relationship and responsibilities wisely, she would seek the kingdom of God and all his righteousness, I have a drive and compassion to my family, friends and enemies to do good toward them, I love to use my gifts he has given me and to allow the beauty I have inside to shine, a value of a virtuous woman is far beyond rubies, now this is what I see and press toward to before the day the lord calls me home to rest, so that I can receive my flowers while I am still in the land of living,

1. God can trust a virtuous woman.
2. A virtuous woman has a pattern of consistent goodness toward her God
3. A virtuous woman is willing to work for her God
4. A virtuous woman make a healthy vessel from the inner satisfaction for her God
5. A virtuous woman makes her home in love and purity for her God that is her first desire of a heart after God.
6. A virtuous woman cares for the physical need and not slothful with the ability God gives her.
7. A virtuous woman wants to be wise in business, a hard worker and commits her excellence in God
8. A virtuous woman wants to be a prayer warrior for God
9. A virtuous woman make good judgment of protection from her God
10. A virtuous woman cares for the poor and compassionate for the needy like her God
11. A virtuous woman plans ahead so that nothing blindside her from God
12. A virtuous woman dresses herself in a properly attired she dress herself to honor her God
13. A virtuous woman is recognize greatly by her husband, merchant, her children, for her excellence, wisdom and kindness what a honor and responsibility God could ever give a woman today, your physical appearance only last for a season, but a Godly, virtuous woman has enduring inner beauty the world could never produce having a Godly virtue, causes everyone to know to praise how bless we are, and this is what God is looking for in men and women today when we do it God s way, we have no need to fail at anything that God put our way.

So aloud God to rebuild you in his own image so that we will not be rottenness to his bones, know that there is no new story under the sun that God has not known or heard but put it out their so that some one can be healed and set free form the chains made from life.

Who can find such a woman? I pray that this is what God finds in me on my Judgment day.

In today generation we need to open up more with our children and let them know of the tricks that the Enemy would try in their life there is no new trick under the sun that the enemy would bring if it did not work with you believe me he would and will try it with the next generation so lets break the chains God gave us brains to open up the knowledge he is giving us in his word and the revelation on how to resist all temptations, you got to let go of the old man so that God can put on the new man. In I Colossians chapter three verses nine and ten tells us to put off the old man with his deeds and put on the new man which is renewed in knowledge after the image of him that created us, Even when you are walking with the lord know that every thing can look good for a while but don't be surprise that Satan is ramping and roaring waiting until he can attack again so be on guard with the whole armor of God,

Christ is looking for committed followers so that we can be good spiritual mentors and leaders.

If you want to know if my trails and tribulations? I would ask you have Jesus returned yet?

All I can tell you is that I am dedicating my life daily to the lord, I am walking on that straight and narrow road, toward eternal life, I am trying to lay all my heavy burdens and trying to be submissive and obedient to God I know that my mind is made up and I will not turn back, I know that this battle is not mine it is and always belong to the lord, His word promise me that in Revelation chapter twenty one verse four and God shall wipe away all Tears from their eyes; and there shall be no more death, neither sorrow, nor crying, neither shall there be any more pain: for the former things are passed away!!! I want to thank and praise God for how he strength me through this whole book, to be able to relieve this God has truly been my Anchor hold, he has took be back and through this like a solider, and I hope and pray someone out there that reads this story realize that God is not a respect of person.

Romans chapter two verse eleven has giving me another chance he has brought me out of darkness and into his marvelous light, truly through the mist of it all I have not always been faithful or true and have done a lot of damage and hurt one that I have love through my own self pity, I have not always trusted God to pull me through even when he had showed me his hand, and surly have not always obeyed him, but check this out" when the devil thought he had sink signed and delivered my feet on sinking sand God snatched me out just in time, for his purpose and plan, he is an on time God!

I am a living witness of the Devine Agape love of God has for us,

Thank You Wonderful Counselor, Prince of Peace The Mighty God>

God has more stories out there, and he wants them to be told, he wants to help your growth in him, build your faith in him, and trust in him.

We overcome by one another testimony!!!

Now that the truth is out concerning by testimony, and my life, I pray that I have reached someone

To come clean come out that hidden closet and stop looking at the trick mirror the enemy set before us, and get it right before it is to late, I don't know how God would have you do it, it might not be In a book but someway the lord will make it known to you, I know that my children will have a lot of question, but I know that the seed that God have in us will make us stronger to help another family, I did not write this story for compassion or pity, God has given me all that I need to over come, what is coming ahead. All I and my family need is your prayers, because the enemy is mad that this had came out, I allowed him to have to much control over my family inherits, and now it is time to let God have full control and start driving us to our destiny,

Some things are in God timing so that it will heal the way it needs to be healed, so don't rush out and give all your goods to the dogs, wait on the lord make sure that it is God that is specking to you, I have tried to write this book for over 15 years and could not, because the parts was not put together yet, to be release, the name of the ministry God has in trust to me is Angel W/Extra Blessings. I did not understand the name until I work in it by and by, the pieces came together, I was Angel W/Extra Blessings I had so much to offer and to bless others with this awesome testimony I could relate in all areas of life and help minister to the souls of God children, I just thank God for his patience that he had on me and all my ups and downs and turn a rounds, he never left me nor did he forsake me through the hot mess. It is so funny how we just do not realize that a family generational curse could follow you through many generations, and keep you in bondage, did you realize when it first happened in reading my story? Well it happened first from my grandmother then my mom then me, so the trick of the enemy stops know, in this family tree from my next generation, and to give you another tip, when my mother past, my uncles came down for the funeral and I loved them just like God had first ordain for me to do, there was not pain or hurt that I felt toward them, I have totally forgiven them I hug them and was not afraid, but happy and glad to see them, the past is behind us and I am moving forward to a awesome life with the lord. Stay tune for the next awesome testimony of the next book God is starting in me. You just don't know how mad the devil is at me for letting go and letting God, so pray!

Love you All!!!

WHO WILL WIPE MY TEARS AWAY?

Who will wipe my tears away?
Who will carry each drop I pray
You reach a hand out and try to understand,
But you see each teardrop I've carried came from man
One who promised to keep me safe?
One who have said I was a disgrace,
Through the years I have learned to tuck my feelings inside,
Each teardrop is where my pain resides.
One by one they do fall
A story behind them all.
I have planned to keep them to myself,
On Gods secret mantel; tucked on a self.
Until I heard an angel say,
Young woman God will wipe each tear away,
From my eyes there shall be no more
The tears that lye behind a human door.
This angel replied no more sorrow, no more crying, no more dying.
There shall be no more pain for former things have passed away.
Because God and only God can wipe my tears away.

Written by
My oldest daughter Theresa Gilford

This poem is dedicated to all my brother and sisters that is
looking for someone to wipe their tears away!
I Love you my brothers and sisters.

THE POWER OF PRAYER

Do you ever have those kinds of days when nothing turns out right?

Where you feel like you're your walking in total darkness and you wish for the light.

When every single step you take it feels like your walking up the hill,

And just continuing with your takes every ounce of will,

Does it sometimes seem like all your hope and dreams will never come to be?

And when you stop to look around your pain is all you see,

Do you ever feel like giving up? From being ragged, used, and worn,

You hurt so much that you wished you were never born?

Whose going to wipe my tears away I say

Sincerely as I pray, don't feel so alone for we all have those days,

Just know that there is someone listening by the way

And waiting on you to do one simple thing, kneel and pray

The power of praying is very great

It is stronger than sin, lust, or even hate.

It can shake the roots of all sin itself until it falls apart

It can humble the strongest soul and it can soften the hardest hearts

Prayer brings hope to those who has no hope and to those who are oppressed

Prayer brings comfort to those who are in pain and to those who are distressed

So when you feel your days been long or you weep for some small loss

Remember the agony that Jesus felt as he suffered on the cross

Remember the crown of thorns on his head

Remember the spear thrust in his side

Remember the nails in his hands and feet

Remember it was all for you! He suffered and died,

Take a long look at your problems and those that Jesus had to bare

You'll find your little problems are nothing to compare

So when you feel down trodden and you need some one who cares

Just bow your head, close your eyes, and experience the power of prayer

Written by my God daughter Nikkia Hudson

ABOUT ME!
WHO I WAS, AND WHO I AM NOW.

I WROTE THIDS BOOK OF MY LIFE TO LET YOU KNOW THAT THIS REALLY HAPPENS IN LIFE STRUGGLES AND IN OUR DREAM FAMILIES TODAY, AND TO LET YOU KNOW THAT YOU CAN OVER COME, NO MATTER WHAT YOU HAVE AND GOING THROUGH IN YOUR LIFE YOU CAN FIND YOUR TRUE IDENTY THROUGH THE LORD, HE WILL AND CAN WIPE YOUR TEARS AWAY IF YOU WOULD JUST GIVE HIM ALL YOUR BURDENS, LAY IT AT HIS FETT AND JUST STEP ASIDE AND WATCH YOUR LIFE BLOOM.

WHO I WAS!

I WAS A LOST SOUL, DAMAGED GOODS, AND FEARFUL OF LIFE AND OTHERS, I HAD NO IDENITY OF WHO I WAS, AND WAS NUMBED THROUGH LIFE'S UPS AND DOWNS, I LIVED IN A LIFE THAT ONLY TOOK THE ROOLERCOASTER THAT TOOK ME UP AND DOWN AND THE MERRY GO ROUND THAT ONLY WENT IN CIRCLES

WHO I AM!

I AM A DEDICATED SERVANT OF THE LORD, A LOYAL WIFE AND A MOTHER OF THREE, A STEP MOTHER OF FIVE AND I HAVE FIVE GRANDCHILDREN, AND FIVE GOD CHILDREN, I AM A SPRITUAL MOTHER TO THE CHILDREN IN MY COMMUNITY, I AM A EVANGELIST IN MY CALLING OF THE LORD TO BE A SERVANT TO HIS PEOPLE, I LOVE

CARING FOR THE PEOPLE IN THE COMMUNITY SUCH AS LOST SOULS, LEADING THEM TO OUR SAVIOUR THE LORD OF MY SOUL AND THE KEEPER OF MY HEART, THE CLAY MAKER AND RENEWER OF MY MIND, I HAVE THE VICYORY THROUGH HIM THAT LOVE ME, I HAVE A TESTIMONY THAT KEEPS ME ON FIRE, I AM WHO HE SAY I AM, A CHILD OF THE ALMIGHTY, PRINCE OF PEACE, THE ONLY ONE THAT CAN BE A PROVIDER, A BATTLE FIGHTER, A GIVER OF PEACE, A HEALER, MY RIGHTEOUSNESS, MY EVER PRESENT ONE, AND MY GOOD SHEPHERD, I AM GOD CHOOSEN VESSEL.

Be Patient with me,

God is not finish with his true servants yet!!

This book is specially dedicated to my Brother Curtis Wright who inspired me to fight through the crowd, and this helped me touch the hem of God's garment'

And two Artists that through their Music Ministry I push toward the mark

Tramaine Hawkins – The Potter House
Yolanda Adams – The Battle Is Not Yours
And to a very special counselor that walked through the fire with me and never let go of my hand! Kathy Melito
Minister Darlene Brown who minister life through her anointed song of praise, I Love You My Sister
I give special Thanks to:
New Zion Deliverance Church
Elder Nothrice Pate
Holy Temple C.O.G.I.C.
New Hope Baptist Church
Book written By Evangelist Earlina Gilford - Weaver
WAIT TILL YOU READ THE NEXT BOOK!!

IT IS NOT OVER UNTIL GOD SAY SO.

I give God all the glory for allowing me to come out and shine
among the mess
Even though I was a victim of physical and sexual abuse and
mental abuse
God has birth a ministry in me to carry out nationwide so it will
send the captive free
And share the victory of healing; I had suffered 35 years of not
knowing that I could breath on my on.

Hallelujah I Am Free!

The Lord Is Carrying Me Through It All

With all I have been through it has been a joy to know that I have revelation now, I learn how to:

- Deal with emotional pain because of the abuse: **Thank You Jesus**
- I understand my responsibility as a child of God: **Thank You Jesus**
- I can over come my addictive behaviors due to my past: **Thank You Jesus**
- I know now that I have unconditional love through him that loves me "God": **Thank You Jesus**

I know that all things works in God's time and it will be right on time, so give him the praise while I still can:
Thank You Jesus
Evangelist Earlina Gilford-Weaver

A child of the lord who had so many trails and tribulations, not Knowing her identity for half of her life, she was broken in so many pieces and did not know where and how it was Going to be put back together, even as she grew into a young adult she felt self worth to her community.

Every one she had came in contact with, shedding tears every where she went, searching for that ultimate one that would and can wipe her tears away, only digging a deeper hole for her purpose in life, through this hurt whelming, heart breaking battle, she stopped and knock on one more doors where she found the lord in 1985 and develop a relationship with him and found love like she never had before, she finally was going to experience and feel what it takes to have the tears wiped away, and have, Earlina has been running for the Lord ever since, what a joy she has found in her life, Her true and only first love, has given her the vision of an angel working and laboring in her true calling and true passion she had all the time, after shed one long tear the lord heard her cry from the power she had within, she picks up her cross to carry it to the end, sharing her testimony to all the corners of the world.

East, West, South, and North, whoever the lord sends her way, Earlina gave birth to the ministries the lord had in her in 2003, with the names the lord provided, Angel W/Extra Blessing, Angel That Give Love, and God Chosen Angels, An out reach ministry that needs to bloom, the Lord Jesus Christ our Savior had died on the cross just for this type of things that need to come alive because he still lives inside of us.

Earlina became an Ordain Minister in 2008. Her passion is doing the lord work that comes from the hidden part of the body the **Heart**! And to open up some outreach ministries one day and serve God's people all over, by just being a Servant and show the true love that would truly help some of the tears in our generation today!

God Gets All The Glory!